MESSIAH
of the
WINEPRESS
Christ and the Red Heifer

MESSIAH
of the
WINEPRESS
Christ and the Red Heifer

KAREN BOREN

Beit Parah Publishing

MESSIAH OF THE WINEPRESS
Copyright ©2002
Beit Parah Publishing
Post Office Box 676
Provo, UT 84603-0676

ISBN 0-9675661-2-6

Cover design:
Paul Springer, Bailey-Montague Graphic Design.

Cover art:
"Christ in a Red Robe" by Minerva K. Teichert
© Intellectual Reserve, Inc.

Back cover photography:
One of Rev. Clyde Lott's Red Angus Cattle, by Karen Boren

Photo on page 23 courtesy Rabbi Chaim Richman
Photos on pages 108 & 109 courtesy Vendyl Jones
All other photographs by Karen Boren

Dedicated to the memory of
Nancy Catlin Honig
who taught me to dare to dream

and

to Teri Williams
who shares my love of the Lord Jesus Christ
and who made this dream come true

Contents

Foreword

For centuries people have longed for the second coming of Christ on the earth. Volumes have been written in hopes of proving to people that all the signs in the earth line up with Scripture, thus revealing His immanent second coming.

For example, the Scripture reveals that one of the signs evident before Christ's return is that "Men shall travel to and fro and knowledge shall increase." If we consider that for 6000 years people traveled the earth on horseback, and now, within just 150 years, we have gone from the car to the airplane to the moon—it is very exciting. We are truly traveling "to and fro." And with the advent of computers, never has there been a time in modern history when knowledge has increased so rapidly.

But there was one sign missing. It truly is the glorious shining jewel that history has been waiting for—the Red Heifer. And now the Red Heifer is here . . . spotless, pure, and perfect.

I have been blessed to know Karen Boren for several years. We met each other because of the magnificent research she has done on the ancient healing oils in the Bible, therapeutic essential oils. Through this process of sharing research with each other over the years, I have gained a very deep respect for her because she leaves no stone unturned and I have found her research to be impeccable.

With all my heart I believe that Karen Boren has been given a special anointing to reveal the message of the Red Heifer to the world. The passion in Karen's heart to study the Red Heifer and her many trips to Israel pursuing truth have led to her brilliant writing on this subject.

This book is not for the weak in heart . . . but it is for everyone sincerely seeking truth and longing for the return of our wonderful Lord and Savior, Yeshua, (Jesus Christ). For in His return is our blessed hope, our continuous joy and our eternal salvation.

May your soul be filled with our Father's great love for you as you read this beautiful book.

— Teri Williams
   Co-Author, Where's The Food and Essential Health Alert,
   Co-Editor, You Can Live!
   Founder of the Essential Oils Healthline research team.

Introduction

In 1997 I was asked to host a talk-radio program about religion on A.M. station KTKK in Salt Lake City. While pondering a name for the show, I came up with *Time of the Signs*. When the station owner asked what I had decided and I told him, he said, "Don't you mean *Signs of the Times?*" No, I said, I wanted to underscore that we are living in the TIME OF THE SIGNS for those who have *eyes to see*.

Think how difficult it was for a believer 100 years ago (or even 50!) to explain just how God would fulfill his word regarding the two witnesses in Jerusalem (Rev. 11:8-12) . . . that everyone in the world would see them resurrected after their bodies lay unburied on the street for three-and-a-half days. *Impossible*, the scoffers challenged. Today we live in an age of instant communication where 2.5 billion people across the globe simultaneously watched Princess Diana's funeral. Now, those particular words in Revelation are completely plausible.

And then there is the quirky fact regarding the Ukrainian word *chernobyl* and wormwood. Peter Lorie, in his book *Revelation: St. John the Divine's Prophecies for the Apocalypse and Beyond,* writes: "The name of the Ukrainian town of Chernobyl, where a nuclear power station in the old Soviet Union first suffered the first meltdown and did so much damage to the areas of land around it and the people that lived there, translates into the herb named wormwood, thus giving us a possible direct connection with nuclear fallout and its results."

When John prophesied in Revelation that a star named Wormwood will fall to earth and contaminate one-third of the waters, not until our age could we ponder the possibility of a nuclear-powered satellite or missile falling to earth wreaking deadly havoc where it lands. Fulfillment of biblical prophecy is indeed being played out in the daily news, but only for those who are watching for the Lord's coming and recognize the abundance of fig leaves!

I worked for a daily newspaper for 12 years. Because of my interest in religion I was blessed to meet and interview some of the end-time players who are on the stage of God's greatest production: The Last Days. I came to understand why Evangelical author Chuck Missler often says that coincidence is not a kosher word. I believe I was where I was supposed to be.

I attended the First Annual Temple Conference at the Jerusalem Hilton in 1992 hosted by Missler, Lambert Dolphin and Don Stewart. That was where I met and interviewed some of the Jewish movers and shakers who are preparing the way for the rebuilding of the Temple in Jerusalem.

The main reason I attended the conference (at great financial sacrifice) was because I had become intrigued by a little-known Old Testament ritual called the Sacrifice of the Red Heifer, and Chuck Missler told me during an interview that it would be one of the discussion topics. As soon as he said that, I knew I had to attend.

This sacrificial rite, found in the Hebrew Bible (Old Testament) in Numbers, chapter 19, is one of the most obscure rituals in all of scripture. You wouldn't be reading this book if you were not aware of how little is known in Christian literature about this topic.

For almost 2,000 years, no heifer was born in the world that met the stringent requirements of this passage in the Torah or First Five Books of Moses. When an all-red calf was born near Haifa, Israel in 1996, the entire world seemed to learn about this heifer and the significance of her birth.

But until newspapers trumpeted the birth of this calf, there was so little known about the Red Heifer that my newspaper web page received hits from around the world from people searching for information simply because I mentioned a story I had written about the search for the Ashes of the Red Heifer.

There is quite a tale about how I was led to study this arcane topic.

On my first trip to Israel in 1985, I stood on the Mount of Olives and listened while tour guide Daniel Rona discussed Numbers 19 and how the Red Heifer was sacrificed on the mount in the time of the First and Second Temple. It was impressed upon my heart on that chill February day that I needed to learn all I could about this sacrifice. What you will read in this book is the result of 17 years of studying, collecting books and articles. From the U.C. Berkeley Library to the Internet to Pomerantz Books in Jerusalem, I have pursued every lead to try to understand how this sacrifice could teach me about Jesus Christ. For no matter how unlikely, I know that all things in scripture testify about and point to the Savior.

The more I searched and prayed, the more I seemed to be led to Jewish sources. I firmly believe that there is no one on this Earth who can understand the Bible better than the Jews. There are Hebrew literary devices and poetical forms in the Bible that have great meaning if you understand them.

I must note that from the age of 13—*Bat Mitzvah!*—I have been drawn to all things Jewish and the State of Israel. At this writing, I have traveled to Israel five times; even serving for three weeks as a *Sar El* volunteer in the Israeli Navy. You will probably not be surprised to learn that my genealogist mother uncovered a Jewish line among our German ancestors named Messinger. My love of Judaism is literally in my blood.

Through my work for the newspaper and my radio show, I became acquainted with a number of biblical scholars from Chuck Missler, Hal Lindsey and the Rev. Clyde Lott, to Dead Sea Scroll scholars Shemaryahu Talmon and Florentino Garcia Martinez; former Baptist minister Vendyl Jones and Rabbi Chaim Richman of the Temple Institute in Jerusalem. The more I studied and talked with different biblical experts, the more I yearned to be taught through my prayers and study. I needed to learn with my heart as well as my mind. It is my belief that those prayers were answered.

I believe in the God of Abraham, Isaac and Jacob and I believe that Jesus Christ is His Only Begotten Son. I search the scriptures knowing that they point me to Christ. I also stand firmly on the word of Jeremiah 33:3: "Call unto me, and I will answer thee, and show thee great and mighty things which thou knowest not."

I testify that we are living in the time of fulfillment of the words of Isaiah and Habbukuk who told us that an era would come when the knowledge of God would cover the earth like waters cover the sea. I also believe that many great things not known before are today being made available to man through the influence of the Holy Spirit. I bless God's Holy Name for sending light and knowledge through study and prayer.

Through my studies with Chuck Missler I was introduced to Christian writer E.W. Bullinger D.D. (1837-1913) who wrote:

> The command to disciples or learners is "Search," "Search the scriptures" (John 5:39). Let us see what we may learn from noting accurately the meaning of the word here translated "Search" (ereuano). It means to trace out, to track, to follow or scent out as a dog or a lion; hence to notice a word, follow it out, see how it is used elsewhere, trace it and track it out in all its usages, and thus learn the mind of the Spirit and the will of God. There is another word used in Acts 17:11, where it says of the Jews of Berea, "These were more noble than those of Thessalonica, in that they received the word with all readiness of mind and searched the scriptures daily whether these things were so." The word here is (anakrino) and it means to divide up; hence, to estimate carefully, judge or sift, and it shows us how, if it be an apostle speaking, or even an angel from heaven, we are to go to the

Word of God, compare it with what He has said, and judge of it accordingly. Then it will be true of us, as it was written of them—"Therefore many of them believed."

As we search the Word of God, we must keep in mind Paul's admonition from Col. 2:16-17 where he reminds us:

Let no man therefore judge you in meat, or in drink, or in respect of an holyday, or of the new moon, or of the sabbath days. Which are a shadow of things to come; but the body is of Christ.

So much of scripture exists simply to typify the works of the Savior. We must study the words and symbols diligently to seek the message of Christ that is contained therein.

I have read, pondered, sifted and prayed to understand how the sacrifice of the Red Heifer is a type or symbol of *Yeshua HaMeshiach*, Jesus the Christ. In this book I have given you the background of ancient use and what is currently happening regarding this sacrifice. The last two chapters of the book are my interpretation of what this arcane sacrifice means to me as a Christian.

It is my opinion that no Christian can write about this sacrifice without looking at it through Jewish tradition. I searched long and hard for each reference. This information seems to fit in my heart. I pray that you will be as the Bereans and put these ideas to the biblical test.

As I studied on my own and with Chuck and Nancy Missler I began to read more and more writers from the late 1800s: C.H. Spurgeon, Adam Clarke, A.W. Pink, Alfred Edersheim and E.W. Bullinger. I also became very well acquainted with the great Jewish commentators: from Rashi and Maimonides, right down to modern Jewish scholars like the late Menachem Schneerson of the *Lubavitchers*, Rabbi Chaim Richman and Rabbi Levi Meier. I have been greatly blessed by these men of God.

You may wonder why I lean mostly on one version of the Bible throughout this book. I can assure you that there is no shortage of Bibles in my library. I have at least 26 different versions ranging from the NIV, Geneva and E.W. Bullinger's *Companion Bible* to Aryah Kaplan's *Living Torah*, the *Five Books of Miriam* and the Hebrew-English *Jerusalem Bible* published in Israel by Koren which is the Bible used by Orthodox Jews.

Most of the biblical quotes in this book are from the King James Version simply because I have come to love the beauty of the translation. Chuck Missler, whose ministry Koinonia House has richly blessed my life, also recommends this version. But there are instances where other translations bring new insights and needed clarification.

I am not a Bible scholar, I have no college degrees to recommend me. I simply love God's Word and have made it my life's priority to study it. If there is anything valuable to this work it is simply because "God hath chosen the foolish things of the world to confound the wise." (1 Cor. 1:27)

And a final note to all you proofreaders out there: I have been tried to be absolutely faithful to quote from references with exactness. If you see *judgement, colour* and *marvellous*, and think they are misspelled, just know that the references came from books printed in England and are correct by British standards.

You may also notice in quotes from Orthodox Jews that the name of Deity is spelled in an unusual way. When you see G-d or L-rd, know that out of reverence for our Father, Jews do not spell out His name. Other times He is called *HaShem*, which is Hebrew for "The Name." In our profanity-laced society, this reverence is very dear to me.

I now humbly offer this study of Numbers 19 as a type of the Atonement of Jesus the Christ. I speak not for any particular denomination; in fact, my studies lean heavily on Jewish and Christian people of many different religions. From Catholic scholars, to Baptist, Evangelicals, Methodists and the late Mormon artist Minerva Teichert who loved the Savior and painted the magnificent cover art—a wide range of Christian believers are represented along with many Jewish scholars and religious leaders.

I humbly pray that my Jewish friends will not take offense in my seeing *Yeshua* in their writings. I acknowledge and apologize for the grief they have suffered at the hands of so-called Christians. But my faith in Christ is my most cherished possession. And my seeing Messianic types in the Hebrew Bible is the greatest compliment I could possibly offer them.

For the opportunities to walk in the Holy Land, the people and the reference books that came my way almost serendipitously, I give glory to God. May we all be blessed to know the Messiah who is coming and to be worthy to stand before Him.

— Karen Boren

Chapter One

Blessed Calf: The Red Heifer of Numbers 19

Signs? What Signs?

A spotless Red Heifer;
A "burdensome stone;"
The nation of Israel left nearly alone;
A union in Europe and
Several "blood moons;"
So—Where are those signs
That His coming is soon?

Earthquakes and famines
All over the place,
Comets and "aliens" —
Is there "life in space"?
Biotechnology,
Computers and cloning;
The earth filled with violence,
Creation is "groaning"!

But relax, there's no hurry;
His coming isn't near!
(Some souls are so blind,
They won't see 'til He's here!)

— Lori Fiechter (used with permission)

The birth of an all-red calf on a kibbutz near Haifa, Israel in late summer of 1996 made headlines around the world when it was announced in May, 1997. In a quieter announcement, known only to Internet patrons and a close network of Christians and Orthodox Jews, a Red Heifer born in Israel was announced on April 8, 2002 by the Temple Institute in Jerusalem.

For those not acquainted with the Bible, these announcements may have been the first time they had heard about the commandment found in Numbers 19 of the Old Testament. It was news to many that Orthodox Jews had been actually searching for a calf to meet those requirements.

Why all the fuss about this *red heifer*? Some Christians say this ritual is something that was done away with by the coming of Jesus Christ. Is it important only to Jews? Is it a sign that the Third Temple will be built? Can it teach us about purity? And does it have any meaning for Christians?

These are the questions I will explore in this book. I have spent many years researching in what became a personal quest. I have become friends with Rev. Clyde Lott, the Mississippi cattle rancher who bred a Red Heifer certified in 1994 by Rabbi Chaim Richman of Jerusalem's Temple Institute. Rev. Lott made an intriguing statement to me as I talked with him about the possibility of me flying to Mississippi to attend a presentation by Rabbi Chaim Richman about this Red Heifer.

Rev. Lott said that his family's involvement with Rabbi Richman was a complete faith walk: "God took us down to nothing. He helped us get to the place where we committed our life to this project. We literally went down to nothing. It was a test to make us completely dependent on Him—He would supply our needs. It's very scary, but we have needs met every day." As Clyde Lott "let go and let God," he found that the money for a plane ticket to Jerusalem would come the very day he needed it. As he sat wondering how he could pay for the flight reservations he had made, a man drove up and told Rev. Lott he had just sold a load of hay and the Lord told him to tithe it to Rev. Lott.

I have been blessed with the same kind of experience as I have written this book. "Just enough, just in time." I am amazed at what the Lord has done for me, but I have to say it has been very difficult indeed.

I look back and marvel at how the Lord placed this burden of learning on my heart and then provided the ways for me to accomplish it. I believe that the Sacrifice of the Red Heifer was a mystery awaiting the right time for its great light to shine forth in the Last Days. This work has been a great honor as well as a burden. I humbly pray that every reader of this book will learn something about the Red Heifer that will teach him or her about God's work through His Son, Jesus Christ.

God Teaches Moses About Purity Through the Sacrifice of the Red Heifer

The commandment to offer the Red Heifer was given to Moses in the wilderness and recorded for all time in the Book of Numbers, chapter 19. The Jewish historian Josephus wrote about the first Sacrifice of the Red Heifer saying that it followed a mourning period after the death of Miriam, the sister of Moses and Aaron:

> . . . and when they had mourned her for thirty days, Moses purified the people after this manner: He brought a heifer that had never been used to the plough or to husbandry, that was complete in all its parts, and entirely of a red colour, at a little distance from the camp, into a place perfectly clean. This heifer was slain by the high priest,

[Josephus errs here, the calf was not slain by Aaron, but by his son Eleazar according to Numbers 19] and her blood sprinkled with his finger seven times before the tabernacle of God; after this, the entire heifer was burnt in that state, together with its skin and entrails; and they threw cedarwood, and hyssop, and scarlet wool, into the midst of the fire; then a clean man gathered all her ashes together, and laid them in a place perfectly clean. When therefore any persons were defiled by a dead body, they put a little of these ashes into spring water, with hyssop, and dipping part of these ashes in it, they sprinkled them with it, both on the third day, and on the seventh, and after that they were clean. This he enjoined them to do also when the tribes should come into their own land.[1]

The Jewish Oral Tradition teaches what Moses learned during his 40 days on Mount Sinai with the Lord and throughout the wilderness experience. Certainly Moses was taught much more than the Ten Commandments. These traditions, carefully preserved by the Jews, clarify many seeming inconsistencies in the sequence of scripture. For instance, in Numbers 7:7, Moses is instructed to cleanse the Levites by sprinkling them with the "water of purification." The water referred to here is most probably the water which was mingled with the Ashes of the Red Heifer, an ordinance not given in the Torah until Numbers 19.

In a modern-day commentary on the Torah (the Five Books of Moses) is this statement: "At Marah, the well of bitterness, Israel is given its first set of divine ordinances, although which ones they were is not specified." This is suggested from Exodus 15:25 where we are told: "there [the Lord] made for them a statute and an ordinance, and there he proved them." The commentary continues with: "The usual translation of *chok umishpat* is 'statute and ordinance.' The Rabbis understood *mishpatim* to be laws that would have validity even without a written Torah . . . while *chukim* are other Torah laws, such as those dealing with the prohibition of pork for food . . . or wearing garments made of wool and flax."[2]

The Midrash (a collection of parables and rabbinic reflections on the Torah) says of *chukim*: "Four Torah laws cannot be explained by human reason but, being divine, demand implicit obedience: to marry one's brother's widow (Deut. 25:5); not to mingle wool and linen in a garment (Deut. 22:11); to perform the rites of the scapegoat (Lev. 16:26, 34); and the red cow. Satan comes and criticizes these statutes as irrational. Know therefore that it was the Creator of the world, the One and Only, who instituted them."[3]

It is Jewish understanding then, that Moses was given certain *chukim* at the time of the healing of the bitter waters of Marah. The *chukim* are the ordinances that man must obey even though he doesn't understand why. The Red Heifer ordinance was given to Moses here at Marah, although it was not recorded until after the rebellion of Korach in Numbers 19.

The Cow and Islam

I find it very intriguing that the Sacrifice of the Red Heifer is referred to in the Qu'ran (the accepted spelling used to be "Koran"), the book holy to Muslims, which they believe was revealed to the Prophet Mohammed by the Angel Gabriel. In the traditional arrangement, the first Sura (chapter) is called "The Cow." N.J. Dawood's translation reads:

> "When Moses said to his people: 'Allah commands you to sacrifice a cow,' they replied: 'Are you making game of us?' 'Allah forbid that I should be so foolish!' he rejoined. 'Call on your Lord,' they said, 'to make known to us what kind of cow she shall be.' Moses replied: 'Your Lord says: 'Let her be neither an old cow nor a young heifer, but in between.' Do, therefore, as you are bidden. 'Call on your Lord,' they said, 'to make known unto us what her colour shall be.' Moses replied: 'Your Lord says: 'Let the cow be yellow, a

rich yellow pleasing to the eye. . . Let her be a healthy cow, not worn out with ploughing the earth or watering the field; a cow free from blemish. . . And they slaughtered a cow, after they had nearly failed to do so. And when you slew a man and then fell out with one another concerning him, Allah made known what you concealed. We said: 'Strike the corpse with a piece of it.' Thus Allah restores the dead to life and shows you His signs, that you may grow in understanding."[4]

In Mohammed's writing about this sacrificial rite, the cow becomes yellow, there is no mention of burning the cow and there is a seeming connection with use of a piece of the slain heifer to raise the dead. Very puzzling and unlike what was given to Moses.

Jews and the Impurity of Death

Regardless of Muslim interpretations, to Jews, if one came in contact with death (walking on a grave, being in a house when someone died, touching a bone) he or she has became "impure" or separated from God. Until this person was sprinkled with spring water (Hebrew: living water) with a small amount of the Ashes of the Red Heifer, they could not worship in the Tabernacle or the Temple. This statute was given to Israel "for ever" and as a "perpetual statute unto them." Because all of Israel since temple times has unavoidably been in contact with death, Orthodox Jews are forbidden to step on the Temple Mount lest they profane where the Holy of Holies once stood. You begin to see that not one person can begin even the most preliminary work on the Temple Mount until they have been purified by the Ashes of the Red Heifer.

The burnt remains of this calf, with the resulting wood ashes from the fire and the ashes from the scarlet wool, hyssop and cedar that were mandated as a part of the sacrifice, were pounded into a fine ash and then stored in three places. The ashes were placed in stone vessels, since stone does not transmit impurity.

The Mishnah is the oral tradition spoken of earlier which was given to Moses at Mount Sinai and transmitted "mouth to ear" until it was written or codified in the Second Century by Rabbi Judah *haNasi* (the prince). It informs us that "They divide [the ashes] in three parts. One is placed on the Rampart, and one is placed on the Mount of Olives, and one was divided among all the [priestly] courses."[5] You might imagine that the ashes would last a long time as only a tiny amount was needed for addition to spring water to make the Waters of Purification (also called the Waters of Separation).

The Second Red Heifer

Tradition says that it wasn't until the time of the return from the Babylonian captivity that another heifer needed to be sacrificed. In Ezra chapter 6 is the story of how Darius renewed the decree of Cyrus to allow the Jews to rebuild the Temple in Jerusalem and how the Temple was dedicated and Passover observed once more. In verses 19-20 we read:

> And the children of the captivity kept the passover upon the fourteenth day of the first month. For the priests and the Levites were purified together, all of them were pure, and killed the passover for all the children of the captivity, and for their brethren the priests, and for themselves. (Emphasis added.)

This verse may be recounting the second sacrifice of a Red Heifer when it speaks of the priests and Levites being "purified together," and Jewish tradition is a second witness. Again from the Mishnah, Parah 3, 5 we find: "And who prepared [the red heifers]? The first did Moses prepare. And the second did Ezra prepare. And five from Ezra onward, the words of R. Meir. And sages say, Seven from Ezra onward. And who prepared them? Simeon the Righteous and Yohanan the High Priest did two each. Elyehoenai b. Haqqof and Hanamel the Egyptian, and Ishmael b. Phiabi did one each."[6]

Word of how a religious Jew saved ashes following the destruction of the Temple in 70 A.D. is found in *The Pharisees* by Louis Finkelstein:

> One of these devoted ritualists had the presence of mind to save the ashes of the last 'red heifer' when the city of Jerusalem was taken by the Romans and its Temple burned. No new heifer could be sacrificed after the fall of the Temple, but the ashes of the last one were preserved for no less than 300 years. As late as the third century C.E., the scholars still 'performed the purification ceremony' in Galilee.[7]

A Scholar for Our Generation

A *Tzaddik* (righteous man) has arisen in our day who is perhaps the most knowledgeable scholar today on the rite of the Red Heifer. He is Rabbi Chaim Richman who lives in Jerusalem. Rabbi Richman has been associated with the Temple Institute for many years, serving as both director and head of research. He has written an important but little-known book titled: *The Mystery of the Red Heifer: Divine Promise of Purity.* Rabbi Richman writes, "The Mishnah teaches that up until the destruction of the Second

Rabbi Chaim Richman

Temple, ashes had been prepared from a total of only nine red heifers." [The rabbi accepts the number the sages offered 'seven from Ezra onward.'] Then he quotes a statement from Maimonides: ". . . and the tenth red heifer will be accomplished by the king, the Messiah; may he be revealed speedily, Amen, May it be God's will." Then Rabbi Richman writes: "With this amazing statement, Maimonides recounts an ancient tradition—that the tenth red heifer is associated with the Messianic Era. Does this perhaps mean that the appearance of a red heifer in these waning end times is an indication, a forerunner of the appearance of the Messiah himself, who will officiate at its preparation? . . . we cannot help but wonder and pray: if there are now red heifers—is ours the era that will need them?"[8]

In Rabbi Richman's book he beautifully explains the concept of impurity that results from contact with death:

> . . . when others must busy themselves with acts of lovingkindness for an empty body whose soul has been removed by God, the priests keep their distance—for that body is now devoid of life. This is the secret of why a dead body defiles! For only life is holy. Once life has departed, it is not the stuff of death itself which renders impurity—but the absence of God-given life. . . Thus the priests who serve in the Temple, itself the source of eternal life—for it is the place of the Shekinah, the Divine Glory of God—must distance themselves from the deception of death. For the impurity rendered by death is the contamination of a false vision, a lie. What men call "death" is nothing more than the bonds of transitory life breaking forth and giving way to eternal life.[9]

Ancient Traditions About the Red Heifer

Knowing about the impurity caused by death also makes certain Jewish customs more understandable—like whitewashing tombs. In the Mishnah it describes what was done on the 15th day of the last month of the civil year (Adar): ". . . and they repair the roads and broadways, and the water reservoirs, and they carry out all public requirements, and they mark out the graves," which is further explained in a note: "By means of lime or whitewash so that the priests and nazarites did not walk over them."[10]

This statute also makes sense of the strange Muslim decision to brick up the "Golden Gate," (also called the "Gate of Mercy" or "Gate Beautiful" on the east side of the Temple Mount, and to place graves in front of it. The Muslim conquerors of Jerusalem knew of a tradition that the Messiah was to come to the Jews through this gate. Since he would be holy like a High Priest, he could not (to their way of understanding the Messiah) come near this defiling area since Cohens or priests cannot enter a graveyard. To this day there is a sign in Jerusalem warning Cohens (descendants of the priestly family of Aaron) not to proceed on the road that goes around the walls of the Old City by the Eastern Gate with its graves. But a tradition in Judaism would allow a priest to disregard this law in carrying out a special deed of kindness.

After the death of Rabbi Akiva, who died as a martyr following the Bar Kochba revolt against Rome, Elijah is said to have come to R. Joshua to help him remove Rabbi Akiva's body from prison and give it an honorable burial. Elijah carried the body on his back to a cave where Rabbi Akiva was interred. R. Joshua said to Elijah, "My master, you said you were a priest, and a priest is forbidden to make himself unclean with a dead body." Elijah let him know that for a loving deed, ceremonial law might conceivably be violated.[11]

When the Messiah comes, He will arrive just in time to save His people in the siege of Jerusalem. (See Zechariah 14:4-5.) The Muslim graves that lie before the Gate of Mercy will hardly be an impediment. And is there a more loving deed than the rescue of His people?

The Lord is ever even-handed in His commandments and always makes sure there is a way for man to be obedient. Since He commanded all of Israel to come up to Jerusalem to observe Passover, He even considered the possible situation where a death might have occurred too close to the date of Passover to allow the full seven days needed for purification. In those cases, there was a "second" Passover, one month later for those who did not have enough time to become pure for the regular holy day. (See Numbers 9:10-11 and 2 Chronicles 30:2.)

Chukkat: A Mystery

Jews believe that only Moses knew what the Lord was doing with this *chukkat,* or statute that must be obeyed even though it is not understood. Why was this commandment difficult to understand? Because those who were impure were made pure by this ritual, while all those who took part in the sacrifice or in the sprinkling of the impure person, were pure to start with and then made impure by participating in the ritual! Even the man renowned for his wisdom, King Solomon, was believed to have said: "All these I have comprehended, but as regards the section dealing with the Red Heifer, I have investigated and inquired and examined: I said: I will get wisdom; but it was far from me. (Ecclesiastes 7:23.)"[12]

If the Sacrifice of the Red Heifer was difficult for the sages of Israel to understand, just imagine what happened when a largely-secular media tried to write about it.

The media around the world are not known for biblical expertise and for a simple example, just how many times have you read in a newspaper article about the Book of *Revelations?* (It's not plural.) Therefore, many errors crept into the reporting of the heifer born in Israel. First, it was often reported that the heifer was of a breed that was believed long-extinct. Wrong! A red heifer is much like a "white buffalo" or an albino. It is simply a very rare occurrence in nature.

In addition to being pure red, the heifer must be the first-born of its mother, it must never have been used for work, put to the plow or even had cloth draped over its back. Pure red is interpreted by the rabbis to mean that two hairs of another color disqualify it. Even the calf's eyelashes and hooves must be of a reddish color and the calf must not be blemished in any manner before it is sacrificed. No scrapes against a fence allowed! Can you see that it is truly miraculous that after almost 2,000 years, a Red Heifer was discovered?

It was also reported that a *paste* was made with ashes and water for purification. You can see yourself from reading the account of Josephus and Numbers 19, that only a small amount of ashes were needed in the water of purification. The ashes were much too precious and rare to be making them into a paste. Besides, how would one *sprinkle* a paste?

"Melody" Is Not Kosher—But Not to Worry!

What was page one news about the heifer's birth, became a minor notice buried on a back page when this heifer sprouted so many white hairs in her tail that she was disqualified. Most web sites have not updated to inform people that this calf named "Melody" is no longer *kosher*.

The news about the heifer no longer being pure red went virtually unnoticed. Here's what was forwarded to me on the Internet by a friend:

The Associated Press/Nando.net "Holy cow! Oops, false alarm." JERUSALEM (January 16, 1998)—Hopes that a red heifer named Melody would be the key to Jewish salvation were dashed Friday after the cow's owner said white hairs have been spotted on her tail. Melody gained world fame in May after Rabbi Shmaria Shore said she was a likely candidate to be the first pure red heifer born in the Holy Land in two millennia . . . Shore, a rabbi at Kfar Hassidim, a religious village in northern Israel, revised his prediction after noticing the white hairs. "The truth is that I had serious doubts about her all along," he said Friday.

But fear not. This is indeed the time for the preparation for rebuilding the Temple in Jerusalem because the Lord sent Israel a Red Heifer two years before Melody saw the light of day. And this pure-red calf was bred by the Pentecostal minister Clyde Lott in Canton, Mississippi.

You will read in a later chapter about this heifer and the resulting friendship between Rev. Lott and Rabbi Chaim Richman.

The details of the historic day the Mississippi calf was verified to be a true Red Heifer can be found in Rabbi Richman's Red Heifer book. His friend, the Rev. Clyde Lott, recalls this momentous event:

At midafternoon on November 11, 1994 the Rabbi walked into our barn in Canton to inspect 4 heifers. Almost immediately, he was drawn to one heifer in the middle stall on the north side of the barn. These heifers had been washed and groomed for the Rabbi. They were immaculately clean, for we wanted the Rabbi to be able to examine the heifers down to the skin, hoofline, the eyebrows and even into the ears. He began to study this particular heifer from the tip of her nose to the tip of her tail. He would back up and then come close to the heifer. This went on for at least 10 minutes. Finally the Rabbi backed up to where my brother was standing outside the stall and looked at him and said, "this is the heifer that will change the world." He later told us that this heifer meets the Biblical requirements of Numbers 19. This was the first time in 2000 years that a red heifer had been verified by a rabbi, meeting all these requirements.[13]

Rabbi Richman certifies the first Red Heifer of this era at Canton, Mississippi in 1994

That particular calf will not qualify now as the Red Heifer. The rabbi writes in his book that while the heifer should be three or four years, one that is older could be used. But any cattle transported to Israel would have to have a stapled ear tag for proof of vaccinations which would render a disqualifying blemish. Therefore, a Red Heifer needs to be born in Israel. So the heifer that was born in Israel in 2002 has a good chance of being the one sacrificed. She may not remain entirely red or escape a blemish though, before three years ensue.

I believe that the heifers born in our time are a sign to the faithful Jews who yearn for a Temple and to faithful Christians who are watching the "signs of the times." There will be more of Clyde Lott's Red Angus heifers that qualify as a Red Heifer. And if God wills, they will be residing in Israel. Again, this will be discussed in detail in Chapter Four.

Gershon Salomon

There was also another heifer reported in 1998 to qualify as a Red Heifer. Gershon Salomon, head of *The Temple Mount and Land of Israel Faithful*, was on a speaking tour of the U.S. in June of 1998 and I heard him tell the Evangelical congregation at Jack Kelley's Meta Tauta Society in Salt Lake City, that another red heifer had been born just north of Jerusalem. News of this heifer is not being shared with the media. Salomon presented a video showing this heifer. The video also showed how religious Jews in Jerusalem observed Passover (April 1998) with a sacrificial lamb.

I was in Israel for this Pesach (Passover) and at the religious *yishuv* where I was staying (*Mitzpeh Yericho* in the West Bank), a lamb was also sacrificed. What a huge "fig leaf" this is! Jews observing this Passover commandment show how deep is their desire to obey God's word whether they have a temple yet or not.

Miracles Upon Miracles: More Red Heifers

While checking out some websites that I visit regularly, I ran across the following update on *The Temple Mount and Land of Israel Faithful*. For several years Salomon's group has attempted to lay a cornerstone on the Temple Mount. In a 1999 update (www.templemountfaithful.org), Salomon reported: ". . . less than a year ago in the Ayalon valley not far from Jerusalem where David defeated Goliath another red heifer was born. Not only have red heifers been born in Israel but also in the United States on the ranches of Zionist Christians, friends and lovers of Israel." There are color photos on the website of the Red Heifer born in Texas on such a ranch. Salomon explained how carefully this special animal must be cared for:

> A red heifer needs to be raised and handled in a very special way like a holy thing which is completely dedicated to G-d. It has to be raised in a very special, clean stall and to be fed with special food, and even to be spoiled. She cannot be raised with other calves and especially not with males. It is forbidden to use her for any work or any other needs of the rancher. . . It is no accident that for almost 2,000 years no red heifers were born and now they are coming one after another, in Israel and on the ranches of friends of Israel.

Yet There Is Another Reason to Worry!

The Lord waited almost 2,000 years to send his Jewish children a calf that meets the stringent requirements needed and now more than one of these heifers is here, without cloning or other bio-technical tricks.

Did these miraculous heifers send people scurrying to their Bibles to study the prophecies? In most cases, the answer is unfortunately, no. One of the saddest scriptures in the entire New Testament is found in Luke 19:43-44 where the Lord tells His people:

> For the days shall come upon thee, that thine enemies shall cast a trench about thee, and compass thee round, and keep thee in on every side. And shall lay thee even with the ground, and thy children within thee; and they shall not leave in thee one stone upon another; <u>because thou knewest not the time of thy visitation</u>. (Emphasis added.)

The words of Daniel 9:25 told the Jews to the very day the exact time of the coming of the Messiah to them. "Know therefore and understand, that from the going forth of the commandment to restore and to build Jerusalem unto the Messiah the Prince shall be seven weeks, and threescore and two weeks: the street shall be built again, and the wall, even in troublous times." Exactly 173,880 days or seven times sixty-nine prophetic years of 360 days elapsed between the one time when the Jews were permitted to rebuild Jerusalem and the wall—from the date of Artaxerses' decree on the 14 of March B.C. 445 to the exact day that Jesus rode into Jerusalem on the donkey and allowed the people to proclaim him the Messiah—on the 6th of April, A.D. 32. See Sir Robert Anderson's *The Coming Prince* (originally published in 1894, reprinted by Kregel Publications, 1996), for the mathematical data.

With regard to His Second Coming, the Lord has not given us the exact day but has warned us to know the time and season. How easy it has been for us to stand in judgment of our Jewish brethren who did not recognize the signs of their visitation. We may find ourselves in a similar situation. So much depends on our knowing God's Word about His Messiah! Are you watching for Him?

---

1. Josephus, *Antiquities of the Jews,* translated by William Whiston, Kregel Publications, 1974, Book Four, page 89.
2. *The Torah: A Modern Translation,* Union of American Hebrew Congregations, New York, 1981, page 497.
3. *Numbers Rabbah,* 19:8, as quoted in *The Torah: A Modern Commentary,* page 1149.
4. *The Koran,* translated by N.J. Dawood, Penguin Books, London, 1988, page 339.
5. *The Mishnah: A New Translation,* Jacob Neusner, Yale University Press, New Haven and London, 1988, pages 1017-1018.
6. Ibid., page 1016.
7. Louis Finkelstein, *The Pharisees: The Sociological Background of Their Faith,* The Jewish Publication Society of America, 1940, Vol. I, page 31.
8. Rabbi Chaim Richman, *The Mystery of the Red Heifer: Divine Promise of Purity,* Jerusalem, Israel, 1997, page 76.
9. Ibid., page 16.
10. *Mishnayoth, Shekalim 1, 1,* Judaic Press, Ltd., Gateshead, England, 1983, page 227.
11. C.G. Montefiore and H. Loewe, *A Rabbinic Anthology,* Schocken Books, New York, 1974, pages 288-287.

Chapter Two

Christians and Jews Look at Numbers 19

For now we see through a glass, darkly; but then face to face: now I know in part; but then I shall know even as also I am known.
—1 Corinthians 12:13

It will be a glorious day when Jews and Christians (as well as the honest in heart of all world religions) will sit at the feet of the Messiah and learn that we are all Children of one God. Jewish mystic tradition has a teaching about this time:

> Said R. Judah: "God will one day reveal the hidden mysteries of the Torah, namely, at the time of the Messiah, because 'the earth shall be full of the knowledge of the Lord like as the waters cover the sea.' (Isa. 11: 9), and as it is written, 'They shall teach no more every man his neighbor and every man his brother, saying, Know the Lord, for they shall all know me, from the least of them to the greatest of them.' " (Jer. 31:34.)[1]

Under the Messiah's divine tutelage, our different traditions will be honed to reflect His visage and His life. I firmly believe that Jews will share knowledge with Christians and Christians will share knowledge with Jews. We will rejoice in teaching each other about *Moshiach* (Hebrew for Messiah) from our unique religious cultures. We will no longer see darkly but will understand what God intended us to learn from His Word. And that new understanding will include the mysterious rite of the Red Heifer!

After years of Red Heifer research, I have a certain respect for the plaintive words of King Solomon, as quoted in the Jewish Midrash:

> All these I have comprehended, but as regards the section dealing with the Red Heifer, I have investigated and inquired and examined: 'I said: I will get wisdom; but it was far from me.'[2]

These words are based on Ecclesiastes 7:23: "All this I have proved by wisdom: I said, I will be wise; but it was far from me." I agree with ancient Jewish commentators who suggested long ago that Solomon was referring to the Sacrifice of the Red Heifer. Jewish tradition also suggests that only Moses was given understanding about what the Red Heifer sacrifice means.

There is an intriguing story in the Midrash about a heathen ridiculing the High Priest, Rabbi Johanan ben Zakkai. The heathen mentions the Red Heifer ritual, saying, "it looks like sorcery to me." Rabbi Zakkai asks the heathen what he does for one that is possessed by the demon of madness. The heathen replies that one must take roots and make a smoke beneath the man and sprinkle water on him, then the demon flies away. Rabbi Zakkai's reply is most interesting:

> R. Johanan said, 'Let your ears hear what your mouth has said [i.e. you are condemned out of your own mouth]. This spirit was a spirit of uncleanness, as it is said, "I will cause the unclean spirit to pass out of the land" (Zech.

13:2). They sprinkle upon him the "waters of separation" (Num. 19:21), and the unclean spirit flies away.' When the heathen had gone, his disciples said to R. Johanan, 'You drove off this man with a reed [i.e. you gave him an inadequate answer], what do you say to us?' He said, 'The dead body does not really defile; the water does not really purify; but God has said, I have ordained an ordinance, I have decreed a decree; it is not permitted to you to transgress it.'[3]

In other words: It doesn't matter how you try to explain it, God has spoken and you will obey!

Rabbi Chaim Richman reiterates this sentiment for modern Jews:

The commandment of the red heifer is one of those ordinances which belong to the category of *chok* (plural, *chukkim*). These are statutes which God decreed that cannot be understood by human reasoning. Rather, He requires that we perform on account of our love and fear for Him. Although we can try to delve into the explanation of these laws, and attempt to find some allusion or sense of the ideas conveyed, we know that ultimately their meaning is beyond our intellectual grasp.[4]

But Jews do wonder. On the "*Or Hadash*" website there is this commentary on the Hebrew words *Zot hukkat haTorah*—this is the ritual law. Regarding Rabbi Johanan's words (see above) that this is the law and must be followed regardless of whether or not it is understood, the following suggestion is made:

Rabbi Yohannan is laying stress on the term *zot* —this. The term may be split into the letter *zayyin* meaning clarity and *ot*—a sign or a symbol. The Sage is telling his students that they may find clarity in the evaluation of the symbolism of the ritual.

I agree that the symbolism will yield great meaning to those who seek it.

So what do Christians make of this sacrifice? We certainly can't ignore it, it is part of scripture and was given for a purpose. In Second Timothy 3:16 we are explicitly told that *all* scripture is given by inspiration of God and is profitable for doctrine. It is definitely important for us to puzzle out the meaning of the types and shadows God has used to convey deep spiritual truths.

Because I have a long commute to my work, I've had many hours to ponder such things. I have been listening to the Bible Broadcasting Network's Dr. David Jeremiah on his radio program, *Turning Point.* I have come to love the portion of a hymn that introduces his teaching. It goes like this: "*Open our ears, Lord, and help us to listen. Open our eyes, Lord, we want to see Jesus.*" These simple, yet profound words can guide us to read the Bible expecting to see Jesus in every chapter and verse. For what are types and shadows except word pictures to teach us about the Master?

So let's look at how beloved teachers, both Jewish and Christian, have sought to understand biblical symbolism.

Christian Commentary on the Red Heifer

The earliest Christian commentary on the Sacrifice of the Red Heifer was made by the Apostle Paul in Hebrews 9:13-14

> For if the blood of bulls and of goats, and the <u>ashes of an heifer</u> sprinkling the unclean, sanctifieth to the purifying of the flesh: How much more shall the blood of Christ, who through the eternal Spirit offered himself without spot to God, purge your conscience from dead works to serve the living God? (Emphasis added.)

Christian commentators and exegetes who followed Paul were quick to see references to Christ in the Red Heifer rite. And appropriately so, because for a Christian, all sacrifices must somehow point to Christ. All things in scripture typify Him and His work.

The Epistle of Barnabas states that through this ritual, God is speaking to us plainly: "The calf is Jesus; the sinful men offering it are those who brought him to be slain."[5]

Augustine (who died in AD 430) wrote that the spotlessness of the heifer and her death outside the camp referred to Christ; that the red color suggested the blood of His passion; cedar, hope; hyssop, faith; and the scarlet represented charity. He also suggested that the dead who cause uncleanliness are man's dead works.

From C.H. Mackintosh's 1880's *Notes on the Pentateuch*, comes this explanation:

> The red heifer is pre-eminently a wilderness-type. It was God's provision for defilements by the way, and it prefigures the death of Christ as a purification for sin, to meet our need in passing through a defiled world home to our eternal rest above.[6]

Perhaps the best summation of what early Christians understood about the symbolism of the Red Heifer was written by Adam Clarke in his 1843 Old Testament commentary:

> Several fathers, as well modern as ancient, profess to understand the whole clearly. 1. The **red** heifer with them signifies **flesh of our Lord**, formed out of an earthly substance. 2. Being **without spot, etc.**, the **infinite holiness** of Christ. 3. The **sex** of the animal, the **infirmity** of our flesh, with which he clothed himself. 4. The **red** colour, his **passion**. 5. Being **unyoked**, his being righteous

in all his conduct, and never **under the yoke of sin**. 6. **Eleazar's** sacrificing the heifer instead of Aaron, ver.3, signifies the **change of the priesthood** from the family of Aaron, in order that a new and more perfect priesthood might take place. 7. **The Red Heifer being taken without the camp** (ver. 3) to be slain, points out the **crucifixion** of our Lord **without the city**. 8. The complete **consuming** of the heifer by fire, the **complete offering** of the whole body and soul of Christ as a sacrifice to God for the sin of man: for as the heifer was **without blemish**, the whole might be offered to God: and as Christ was **immaculate**, his whole body and soul were made a sacrifice for sin. 9. As the fire of this sacrifice **ascended** up to God, so it points out the **resurrection** and **ascension** of our blessed Lord. 10. And as the **ashes** of the victim communicated a legal purity to those who were defiled, so true **repentance**, signified by those **ashes**, is necessary for the expiation of the offenses committed after baptism.[7] (Emphasis in the original.)

In Chapter One, we read the account from Josephus about the first sacrifice of the Red Heifer. There is yet another probable discussion of this rite in the Jewish historian's works. Christian prophecy teacher J.R. Church mentioned this obscure reference in Josephus, so I looked it up:

Thus also, before the Jews' rebellion, and before those great commotions which preceded the war, when the people were come in great crowds to the feast of the unleavened bread, on the eighth day of the month Xanthicus [Nisan] and at the ninth hour of the night, so great a light shone round the altar and the holy house, that it appeared to be bright, day-time; which light lasted for half an hour. This light seemed to be a good sign to the unskilful, [sic] but was so interpreted by the sacred scribes as to portend those events which followed immediately upon it. At the same festival also, <u>a heifer, as she was led by the high priest to be sacrificed, brought forth a lamb in the midst of the temple.</u>[8] (Emphasis added.)

A heifer would have been led through Temple courtyards by the High Priest only on one occasion that I am aware of: the sacrificing of a Red Heifer. What Josephus relates here can only be recognized as a miracle, if indeed, it happened. (And R.C. Sproul has written: "The reference to a heifer giving birth to a lamb is bizarre indeed, to the point of raising doubts about Josephus's accuracy as a historian."[9]) Josephus was detailing a number of strange occurrences that preceded the terrible destruction of the Romans. Tuck this possible occurence regarding a heifer and a lamb away in your mind for further discussion below.

You may also consider the connections that Jewish writers made between Aaron's Golden Calf and the subsequent Red Heifer. In volume four of *The Zohar* (page 399) it reads: "Aaron was commanded to offer a calf, to atone for the sin of that other calf which Aaron made. . ." Rabbi Chaim Richman agrees in the book he has written about the Red Heifer for he writes: ". . . the red heifer serves to atone for the spiritual chaos brought into the world through the golden calf."

After these few suggestions about the general meaning of this sacrifice, I would like to delve into the meaning of each component of the ritual. And then I will conclude this chapter with an incredibly beautiful explanation of this ancient ritual by Rabbi Levi Meier.

Parah Adumah: The Red Heifer

The Hebrew for "Red Heifer" is *parah adumah. Parah,* simply means female calf, but there is another word, *eglah,* that means female calf. *Eglah* is used 12 times. *Parah* is used 7 times, six in Numbers 19 where the Red Heifer is mandated, and once more in Hosea 4:16 where the Lord says:

"For Israel slideth back as a backsliding heifer: now the Lord will feed them as a lamb in a large place."

I find it significant that this rite which will yet be performed on behalf of Judah, is rhetorically connected to this promise where the Lord says He will change Israel from a backsliding heifer to a carefully cared for lamb. Perhaps there is an echo of prophecy in the tale Josephus told of a heifer bringing forth a lamb.

The Hebrew word used for "red" is *adumah*. In the Anchor commentary on this chapter, Baruch A. Levine notes that "the adjective *adom* itself may be related to dam 'blood.' "[10]

In I Samuel 16:12 the young David is described as "ruddy, and withal of a beautiful countenance." The Hebrew word for ruddy used here is *admoni*. In the Song of Solomon where it says "my beloved is white and ruddy," the Hebrew word is *adom*. In Genesis 25:25 Esau is described at birth as "and the first came out red." The Zohar says that "one day God will put on a red robe and take a red sword to take vengeance on the ruddy one [Esau]."[11]

Getting back to the Red Heifer, Adam Clarke noted that: "The Hebrews generally sacrificed males, no matter what colour; but here a heifer of a red colour, is ordered. The reason of these circumstances is not very well known." With a nod to Clarke's great contributions to biblical understanding, his remark that the sex of the animal referred to "the infirmity of our flesh," strays from the mark and I will suggest symbolism that does not denigrate the daughters of God. And in Chapters Six and Seven, I will explain in depth two theories that relate to the color red.

We will speak more of color as we discuss "scarlet wool" below, but for now, make a mental note that God has marked the Sacrifice of the Red Heifer as especially significant by its unusual requirements beginning with its color.

A Firstborn *Heifer*

Many commentators believe that this female sacrifice suggests that the ritual is life-giving. The Hebrew word for salvation is Yeshuah, a feminine word (Strong's No. 3444). This is the very meaning of the Hebrew name of Jesus!

As I discussed the Red Heifer with Bible-loving friends, Donna Nielsen suggested this: "A woman typifies Christ in giving birth to life. The red suggests His blood shed to bring forth life."

In their commentary on the Old Testament, C.F. Keil and F. Delitzch write:

> The sacrificial animal was not to be a bullock, as in the case of the ordinary sin-offerings of the congregation (Lev. iv. 14), but a female, because the female sex is the bearer of life (Gen. iii. 20), a *parah*, i.e. lit. <u>the fruit bringing</u>. (Emphasis added.)[12]

As our modern world loses its sensitivity to the sanctity of life, women should reverence and rejoice in the God-given blessing of bringing life into the world. In this way, a woman is indeed typifying the mission of Christ as the bearer of life—she for this world, and Christ, for Life Eternal.

"And the Priest Shall Take Cedar Wood"

The cedar trees of Lebanon were used for Solomon's Temple and can represent the upright and stalwart as represented by Psalm 92:12 where it says: "The righteous shall flourish like the palm tree: he shall grow like a cedar in Lebanon."

But the deadly sin of pride is also represented by cedar. Isaiah writes that the day of the Lord shall fall upon "every one that is proud and lofty, and upon every one that is lifted up; and he shall be brought low: And upon all the cedars of Lebanon, that are high and lifted up, and upon all the oaks of Bashan." (Isaiah 2:12-13)

In the Talmud is recorded another mention of cedar:

> R. Eleazar, son of R. Simeon entered [the Beth Hamidrash] and expounded thus, "A man should always be gentle as the reed and let him never be unyielding as the cedar. And for this reason the reed merited that of it should be made a pen for the writing of the Law, Phylacteries and Mezuzoth."[13]

Hyssop

The hyssop plant was used to smear the blood of the Passover Lamb on the doorposts and lintels of Israelite houses in Egypt when the most fearful plague swept over Egypt: the death of the firstborn. Exodus 2:22 says:

> For the Lord will pass through to smite the Egyptians; and when he seeth the blood upon the lintel, and on the two side posts, the Lord will pass over the door and will not suffer the destroyer to come in unto your houses to smite you.

The combined use of cedar, hyssop and scarlet wool was first mandated by God in Leviticus 14:4 in the cleansing ritual for lepers. The Jewish scholar Rashi commented about humility and pride in regard to these items: "Rashi asks, 'How shall the leper become purified?' He answers, 'He shall humble himself to become as lowly as the scarlet (literally, 'worm') and the hyssop (the lowest plant).' "[14]

It may be significant to also note that in 1 Kings 4:33, Solomon's wisdom and understanding are celebrated with these words: "And he spake of trees, from the **cedar tree** that is in Lebanon even unto the **hyssop** that springeth out of the wall." (Emphasis added.) The mighty cedar and the lowly hyssop together are needed for the cleansing rites for the leper and for those contaminated by death.

King David's anguished prayer of repentance in Psalm 51 includes these words in verse 7:

"Purge me with hyssop, and I shall be clean: wash me and I shall be whiter than snow."

In the first nine verses of this psalm, I see a beautiful chiasmus, two parallel phrases, the second in inverted order. This literary device was used to emphasize something important:

A. Blot out my transgression (verse 1)
  B. Wash me (verse 2)
    C. Cleanse me (verse 2)
    C. Purge me (verse 7)
  B. Wash me (verse 7)
A. Blot out mine iniquities (verse 9)

When verse 7 (see above) was paraphrased into Chaldee (Aramaic), a connection was made with the Sacrifice of the Red Heifer: "Thou wilt sprinkle me like the priest, which sprinkleth the unclean with the purifying waters, with hyssop, with the ashes of an heifer, and I shall be clean."[15]

I believe that hyssop will be used to sprinkle the "clean water" of Ezekiel 36:25 when the Lord will cleanse Israel and give them a new heart. Is it a coincidence that hyssop has antiseptic qualities?

Grant R. Jeffrey writes: ". . . hyssop oil is actually a very effective antiseptic and antibacterial agent. Hyssop oil contains 50 percent carvacrol which is an antifungal and antibacterial agent still used in medicine, according to the book, *None of These Diseases*."[16]

Scarlet Wool

The color scarlet was obtained in ancient Israel by crushing a worm from oak trees. Herbert Lockyer notes the significant fact that the word for scarlet is actually "worm" from which the scarlet dye is extracted. He finds this word in Job 25:6, "The son of man, which is a worm," and Psalm 22:6: "I am a worm, and no man." Then he writes:

The scarlet dye is derived from a particular insect or worm called by naturalists *coccus ilicis*, which is found in large quantities on certain species of oak. The Arabic name of this insect is '*Kermes*' the root of our word 'crimson.' How blessed is the truth taught here! In that great messianic Psalm, Christ declares that He is 'a worm and no man,' which implies that He was not only self-abased, insignificant, weak and despised when He came to earth, but that **He was the 'coccus ilicis' of God from which the precious crimson or scarlet blood was extracted, and which is efficacious to change the scarlet color of our sins into the pure whiteness of the wool and snow** (Isa. 1:18.)[17] [Emphasis added.]

There is more to the haunting words of Psalm 22: "I am a worm, and no man; a reproach of men, and despised among the people" than just the scarlet worm.

The Hebrew word for worm is *tolah* or *tola'ah*. To show how completely, how mysteriously, even the humblest prophetic word is fulfilled, comes this sad report. Samuel Sandmel in his book, *We Jews and Jesus*, tells about a disparaging work about Jesus called *Toledot Jeshu*, possibly from the sixth century. He talks about the "lamentable contents" of the book which were widely circulated among Jews of the Middle Ages in answer to the unChrist-like persecution heaped upon the Jews by so-called Christians. Sandmel writes:

They customarily referred to Jesus by the Hebrew word talui, 'the hanged one,' and as Jews moved about and changed pronunciation, the two consonants remained unchanged, but the vowels underwent permutation and the resultant forms have been '**tola**' or '**toyla**,' or the like.[18] (Emphasis added.)

How incredible, that hundreds and hundreds of years after Christ, He would be called *tola* or "worm" as spoken of in Psalm 22 by a people who no longer were sure of the Hebrew words they spoke. (It will grieve my heart if what I write invokes anti-Semitism. Please do not harbor any ill feelings for people who do not accept Christ as the Messiah. How often do you hear His name profaned in "Christian" culture? And we do not have the excuse that the Lord has blinded us to Him for now. *"He hath blinded their eyes, and hardened their heart; that they should not see with their eyes, nor understand with their heart, and be converted and I should heal them." John 12:40.*)

There is another scriptural connection with this deep red color of Numbers 19. In a sweet book called *Color in Scripture* by D.L. Higginbotham, there is a surprising connection with the tale of Rahab of Jericho. Rahab hid the Israelite spies and for her kindness, her family was saved by her putting a "scarlet line" in her window. Higginbotham makes a connection with the red blood of the Passover lamb smeared on the doorways of the Israelites in Egypt saying, "Both were a shadow of the blood ultimately shed by Christ for the human race." Then she writes this:

> The Hebrew word for "line" here is *tiqvah*. Every other occurrence of the word is translated "hope" or "expectation." The word "hope" is given further illumination in Hebrews 11:1: "Now faith is the substance of things hoped for." Apparently, faith is associated with hope. So here we have this line as a picture of the faith that saved Rahab, as well as the first-born of the children of Israel. Their all-important faith in these red symbols were but shadows of the ultimate faith in the precious blood of Christ which "saves" us today. In addition, the scarlet line is a picture of a blood line because Rahab is an ancestor of Christ Himself (Matthew 1:5).[19]

So the "scarlet line of hope" meant life to Rahab and points us to the Savior today. He is our Hope of salvation. This scarlet "line" continued to have meaning in Jewish sources. In the 1896 edition of Dr. William Smith's Dictionary of the Bible (page 844) is a discussion on *Tephillin* or phylacteries, the small boxes containing scripture that were strapped on the left arm and on the forehead during prayers.

The *tephillin* would obviously mark one as a practicing Jew. So an early edition of Smith's dictionary notes: "In times of persecution a <u>red thread</u> was worn instead." (Emphasis added.) At Jewish "Kabbalah Centres" one can purchase "red string" which comes from Israel and supposedly protects one from evil.

The last time I was in Israel, a woman at the Western Wall was seeking funds for the poor and in return for a donation, she tied a red thread about my wrist and placing her hand on my head, prayed for me. I would say we both believe in the efficacy of that scarlet line of hope!

In Alfred Edersheim's *The Temple: Its Ministry and Services,* he discusses a <u>scarlet line</u> around the altar of the Temple.

> A red line all around the middle of the altar marked that *above* it the blood of sacrifices intended to be eaten, *below* it the blood of sacrifices wholly consumed, was to be sprinkled.[20] (Emphasis in the original.)

(You may also wish to read the definitive Jewish reference to this scarlet line in Adin Steinsaltz's *The Talmud: A Reference Guide,* page 188.)

Whether one speaks of the bloodlines of Christ (Rahab), the scarlet thread used to determine birthright (the twins sons of Judah and Tamar in Genesis 38:28) or the scarlet line on the Temple altar, the Hope of Israel is in the blood of Jesus Christ. In fact, Richard Booker writes that:

> From Genesis to Revelation, the Bible tells one story. The story is that God has entered into a BLOOD COVENANT

with man through the Lord Jesus Christ. . . The blood covenant is the "scarlet thread" that runs through the entire Bible.[21] (Emphasis in the original.)

The Ashes

I learned the most amazing thing from my beloved E.W. Bullinger. (I am so grateful for this man's scholarship and love of Christ.) He wrote about the translators of the King James Version in regards to Psalm 20:3 where it reads "accept thy burnt sacrifice" and then commented:

> But they explain in the margin that the Hebrew rendered 'accept' means to 'turn to ashes' ; because that was the way in which the Lord accepted a Sacrifice. He *turned it to ashes,* by causing Divine fire to fall from the heavens and consume it.[22] (Emphasis added.)

In his commentary on Numbers 1-20, biblical scholar Baruch Levine notes an unusual aspect of this sacrifice. He writes: "The entire cow, even including its blood, was to be burned as the priest watched. Nowhere else in Torah ritual do we find the explicit requirements of burning the blood of ritual victim."[23] (Emphasis added.) I believe the uniqueness of the Red Heifer sacrifice and its blood "being accepted" by being turned to ash points to Jesus Christ and His offering of His life's blood to cover our sins.

There is an interesting fact about the Hebrew word for "ashes" in Numbers 19:17. In this verse, instead of *eper* ("ash") we find the word *aper* which is Hebrew for "dust." I suggest that we might make a connection with the two times "dust and ashes" are used in scripture: by Abraham in Genesis 18:27 and by Job in Job 42:6. Without the Atonement of Christ, we would all be but *dust and ashes* with no hope of resurrection and eternal life. Remember that David spoke of dust in the heart-wrenching description of Christ's crucifixion in Psalm 22 where under the guidance of the Holy Spirit, he wrote: ". . . thou hast brought me down into the dust of death."

Rabbi Richman also made a connection from the word *ashes*. In his Red Heifer book he quotes the sages who said that God told Abraham:

> In the merit of these words you have spoken—"I am but dust and ashes"—I will give your children a commandment they will perform through ashes, and by your life, they will receive atonement through it." (Similarly, on the verse which states "Who can count the dust of Jacob?" Numbers 23:10, the sages reflected: "who can count the merits of the Divine commandments they fulfill with dust?"[24]

Perhaps the most intriguing mention of the word *dust* is in Numbers 5:14-31 where the ritual trial of the *Sotah* or wife suspected of infidelity is outlined. In the Henry W. Soltau book on the Tabernacle, he observes that the floor of the Tabernacle is mentioned only once in the Bible:

> . . . in connection with that remarkable ordeal to which a wife was subjected, if the spirit of jealousy came upon her husband. The priest was commanded to take holy water in an earthen vessel, and into it some of the <u>dust</u> that formed the floor of the tabernacle. He then wrote certain fearful curses in a book, and blotted them out with this water, so that it was as it were pervaded with these curses. The suspected wife stood uncovered before God . . . and the woman drank the water, which if she was guilty, became bitter within her, and caused corruption and curse to be made manifest in her body. The jealous husband taking this course, freed himself from any participation in her iniquity. The woman if guilty, alone bore it, and was a curse among her people. (Emphasis added.)

Soltau made the most beautiful connection with the Savior. He noted that Israel was described as the wife of Jehovah as a type. She was suffering the fearful judgment of His wrath and the fury of His jealousy because she had turned her heart from Him. Then he added:

> The Husband, instead of clearing Himself from the iniquity of His wife, by allowing her to drink the bitter water, has Himself taken the cup, and drained it to the dregs. God, in the fire of his jealousy, because of man's departure in heart from Him, mingled a cup of wrath and indignation, and placed it in the hands of His own beloved Son. "The cup which my Father hath given me, shall I not drink it?" O what a draught did that cup contain! Holy water, mixed with dust and curses, God's holy indignation against sin . . . He refused the vinegar and gall at the hands of man, when He had tasted it. But He drank "the water of gall," and the "wine of astonishment" from the hands of God.[25]

Because the last connection with the word "ashes" approaches the grief and horror of the Holocaust, I humbly add my faith and hope to those found in Isaiah 61:3 where it is promised:

> To appoint unto them that mourn in Zion, to give unto them beauty for ashes, the oil of joy for mourning, the garment of praise for the spirit of heaviness; that they might be called trees of righteousness, the planting of the Lord, that he might be glorified. (Emphasis added.)

To my cherished friends who lost loved ones in the fires of the Holocaust, the Holy One of Israel will restore them to you. I testify to you with Isaiah (25:8):

He will swallow up death in victory; and the Lord God will wipe away tears from off all faces and the rebuke of his people shall he take away from off all the earth; for the Lord hath spoken it.

The Waters of Shiloah

It has been suggested that just as the ashes in this sacrifice represent death, so the water used represents life. In Jerusalem, the Red Heifer rite of purifying from corpse uncleanness used water from a specific pool of spring water. The trouble is, you will see this pool designated as: the Pool of Siloam, or Siloach or Siloah. To make it even more confusing, in Nehemiah 3:15 there is yet another spelling—Shelah.

In Adam Clarke's commentary on the Old Testament, he notes that Siloam is the Greek pronunciation of the Hebrew *Siloah* or *Siloh*. One can go around and around through dictionaries and word studies, but I believe that the word should read "Shiloh."

The Messianic name "Shiloh" is found only once—in Genesis 49:10 where Jacob's prophecy to his son Judah reads: "The sceptre shall not depart from Judah, nor a lawgiver from between his feet, until Shiloh come; and unto him shall the gathering of the people be."

Christians and the early Jewish writers agreed that Shiloh is a Messianic reference. What the word itself means will be discussed below, but I want you to consider an insight I learned from *Turning Point*, the radio ministry of Dr. David Jeremiah heard on the Bible Broadcasting Network (BBN). Dr. Jeremiah suggested that when Jacob wrestled with the "man" (who many believe was the pre-incarnate Christ) who blessed him, after Jacob asked what the "man's" name was, he was told it was *Shiloh*. (This must be deduced from the text since it is not written there.) How else could Jacob have known that a name of Messiah was Shiloh when he blessed Judah? And why else would Jacob call this place the sacred name of Peniel where he saw "God face to face" unless it was the Messiah Himself that Jacob wrestled with?

One of the greatest of Jewish teachers, Rabbi Solomon ben Isaac, known by the acronym Rashi, wrote that the phrase "until Shiloh come" means: "until the King Messiah will come, whose will be the kingdom." Evangelical author Chuck Missler has a wonderful paper titled "Until Shiloh Comes" on a website called "The Y Files" (www.yfiles.com). He adds the following rabbinical references:

Chuck and Nancy Missler

> In the Targum Onkelos it states: 'The transmission of domain shall not cease from the house of Judah, nor the scribe from his children's children, forever, **until Messiah comes**' In the Targum Pseudo-Jonathan it states: 'Kings and rulers shall not cease from the house of Judah . . . **until King Messiah comes**.' The Targum Yerushalmi states: 'Kings shall not cease from the house of Judah . . . **until the coming of the King Messiah** . . . to whom all the dominions of the earth shall become subservient.' " (Missler's emphasis.)

A debate over the meaning of the word Shiloh and its Messianic implications has raged over the millennia. *A New Standard Bible Dictionary*, (Funk & Wagnalls Co., 1926) notes that the phrase "until Shiloh comes" [is] an enigmatical clause in Gen. 49:10 which has taxed the ingenuity of interpreters in all ages." A suggestion is made here that perhaps Shiloh points to the Hebrew word *shelloh* (short for asher lo, 'that which is to or for him'). This does not resonate with me.

I believe the word means *Sent* and that the title of this pool and the Messianic title "Shiloh" may be one and the same. And the great clue to understanding this is found in the Gospel of John.

When the Apostle John mentioned the Pool of Siloam he added: "which is by interpretation, **Sent**." (John 9:7, emphasis added.) John obviously recognized the word "sent" as a Messianic title because he uses the word 42 times in his Gospel! Bullinger would look at 42 as 6 times 7 and in his book, *Number in Scripture*, he writes explaining the significance of six and seven in the genealogies of Jesus Christ:

> . . . while Jesus is the 77th name in the line which comes through Nathan, it is the 66th name in the line which comes through Solomon. When we remember that six is the human number, and seven the Divine, can we doubt that we are thus pointed to the fact that Jesus was both Son of God and Son of Man?[26]

John's witness of Christ is pointing to the uniqueness of the word "sent" by his use of it 42 times. What is the special meaning of this word?

Adam Clarke's commentary on Genesis has a marvelous exegesis that tells us *sent* is "consequently derived from *shalach*, to send, John 9:7.

> Our Lord thus assuming to himself his two leading titles of MESSIAH, signifying anointed and SHILOH, sent forth or delegated from God; as he had done before at the opening of his mission: "The spirit of the Lord is upon me, because he hath <u>anointed</u> me to preach the Gospel to the poor; he hath <u>sent</u> me forth to heal the broken-hearted," &c; Luke 4:18. (Emphasis added.)

Clarke quotes a "Dr. Hales" in this section of his commentary. In Hales' *A New Analysis of Chronology*, (two volumes, 1809-10 and that's all that Clarke tells us about this author and his work) Dr. Hales had made a connection (called a "rhetorical link") with the *send* found in Exodus 3:10:

... [W]here shall we find [Christ's] mission or apostleship (the word apostle means sent!) foretold except in Jacob's prophecy of Shiloh? which was evidently so understood by Moses when God offered to send him as his ambassador to Pharoah, and he declined at first the arduous mission: 'O my Lord, send I pray thee by the hand of Him whom thou wilt send' or by the promised Shiloh.

Dr. Hales continues: "Here then we find the true meaning and derivation of the much disputed term *Shiloh* in this prophecy of Jacob, which is fortunately preserved by the *Vulgate*, rendering *qui mittendus est, he that is to be sent*, and also by a rabbinical comment on Deut. xxii.7: 'If you keep this precept, you hasten the coming of the *Messiah*, who is called SENT.' "[27]

I believe that Moses himself is defining Shiloh for us in this foreshadowing of "The Sent One," Jesus Christ, when he uses the words "Him Whom Thou Wilt Send."

There may be one more significant "rhetorical link." When I was studying M.R. Vincent's *Word Studies in the New Testament*, I read the following about the Pool of Siloam:

The site is clearly identified in a recess at the south eastern termination of Zion, near the junction of the valley of Tyropeon with that of the Kidron. According to Dr. Thomson it is a parallelogram about fifty-three feet long and eighteen feet wide, and in its perfect condition must have been nearly twenty feet deep. It is thus the smallest of all the Jerusalem pools. The water flows into it through a subterranean conduit from the Fountain of the Virgin, and the waters are marked by an ebb and flow. Dr. Robinson witnessed a **rise and fall** of one foot in ten minutes.[28]

I emphasized the words "rise and fall" because they immediately reminded me of Luke 2:34 where Simeon holds the Christ Child in his arms and prophesied: "Behold, this child is set for the fall and rising again of many in Israel; and for a sign which shall be spoken against." Remember that Isaiah foretold the rejection of Christ by Israel in these terms:

> Forasmuch as this people refuseth the waters of Shiloah that go softly, and rejoice in Rezin and Remaliah's son; Now therefore, behold, the Lord bringeth up upon them the waters of the river, strong and many, even the king of Assyria, and all his glory; and he shall come up over all his channels, and go over all his banks. Isaiah 8:6-7.

Christ said He is the Living Water. I believe this scripture also tells us that He is Shiloh and His waters flow softly. (He does not force us to believe in Him) Those "waters" will either raise up or cast down man—depending upon man confessing that Jesus is the Christ, the Son of God.

M.R. Vincent points out yet another intriguing link between Christ and the Pool of Siloam:

> SENT: The Hebrew word means outflow (of waters); *missio*, probably with reference to the fact that the temple mount sends forth its spring-waters. Many expositors find a typical significance in the fact of Christ's working through the pool of this name. Thus Milligan and Moulton, after noting the fact that the water was drawn from this pool for pouring upon the altar during the Feast of Tabernacles; that it was associated with the "wells of salvation" (Isaiah 12:3); and that the pouring out of the water symbolized the effusion of spiritual blessing in the days of the Messiah, go on to say: "With the most natural interest, therefore, the Evangelist observes that its very

name corresponds to the Messiah; and by pointing out this fact indicates to us what was the object of Jesus in sending the man to these waters."[29]

Gershon Salomon's Temple Mount Faithful website posted word that in the May 15, 1999 edition of the Israeli newspaper, HaTsofer, it was reported from a Muslim source that "water had started to flow from the rock on the Temple Mount" and that "Arabs on the Temple Mount have done everything possible to stop the flow of water, including by means of special pumps that they had brought in for the purpose." More recently, water has been slowly leaking from stones in the Western Wall.

If these incidents turn out to be more than just rumor, perhaps the waters of the Temple Mount are being prepared for the day of the prophecy of Ezekiel 47:11-12 when waters will issue forth from the Temple and heal the Dead Sea.

The Feast Of Tabernacles

There was another special rite, in addition to the Red Heifer Sacrifice, associated with the water from this pool. In *The Odyssey of the Third Temple* by Rabbi Yisrael Ariel and Rabbi Chaim Richman, they write:

> One of the main directives for the holiday of Sukkot [Tabernacles] is the commandment: "And you shall be glad on your holiday, and you shall be joyful." (Deut. 16:14) Indeed, the pilgrims who arrived in Jerusalem at the Temple's courtyard came to rejoice. The focus of this rejoicing was the ceremony surrounding the commandment to pour water on the altar—the water of libation. During this event, which mainly took place in the Women's Court, the Levites sang and played on many instruments. The Rabbis testify of the events of the water libation from the days of the Second Temple, describing the great joy of the

ceremony: "Whoever has not seen the celebration of the water libation—has never experienced true joy in his life." (Mishnah tractate Sukkah, Chapter 5).[30]

At dawn, a priest, accompanied by a large crowd, filled a golden pitcher with the spring water of Shiloach. The group ascended to the Temple where the water was poured into a silver cup at one corner of the altar. Rabbi Ariel connected this ceremony with the promise of rainfall in the coming year. Jewish sages believed that on a

R. Richman discusses Temple vessels at the Temple Institute

symbolic level, this ceremony also referred to receiving inspiration—the outpouring of *Ruach Eloheim*, the Spirit of God.

The "pouring out of the water" was associated with Isaiah 12:3 where it says: "Therefore with joy shall ye draw water out of the wells of salvation."

Biblical scholar Alfred Edersheim wrote beautifully about this ceremony and the day when the Master Teacher, who had declared Himself the true "Living Water," spoke to the people in Jerusalem's Temple:

> It was on that day, after the priest had returned from Siloam with his golden pitcher, and for the last time poured its contents to the base of the altar; after the "Hallel" had been sung to the sounds of the flute, the people responding and worshiping as the priests three times drew the threefold blasts from their silver trumpets—just when the interest of the people had been raised to its highest pitch, that, from amidst the mass of worshipers, who were waving towards the altar quite a forest of leafy branches as the last words of Psalm 118 were

chanted—a voice was raised which resounded through the Temple, startled the multitude, and carried fear and hatred to the hearts of their leaders. It was Jesus, who "stood and cried, saying, If any man thirst, let him come unto Me, and drink." Then by faith in Him should each one truly become like the Pool of Siloam, and from his innermost being "rivers of living water flow." (John 7:37-38)[31]

What joy it brought me to understand the meaning of this pool's name! For the Savior is telling me that through faith in Him, I could have the rivers of Living Water flow from my heart as they flow from the Sent One. I especially love the New Living Translation's paraphrase of John 7:37: "For the scriptures declare that rivers of living water will flow from the heart of those who believe in me."

Ezekiel's Clean Water

The last connection with "water" is an important one. The yearly reading of Numbers 19 and the Sacrifice of the Red Heifer has been connected by Jews to a section of Ezekiel. Along with each weekly Torah portion read in the synagogue, they also read a section of the Hebrew Bible. The Numbers 19 complementary reading, called a *haftorah*, is Ezekiel 37:16-38 where the Lord promises Israel:

> And I will sprinkle clean water upon you, and ye shall be clean; from all your uncleannesses, and from all your idols, will I cleanse you. A new heart also will I give you, and a new spirit will I put within you; and I will take away the stony heart out of your flesh, and I will give you a heart of flesh. And I will put My spirit within you, and cause you to walk in Mine ordinances, and do them. And ye shall dwell in the land that I gave to your fathers; and ye shall be My people, and I will be your God. (verses 25-28)

The editor of the Soncino Edition of *The Pentateuch and Haftorahs*, Dr. J.H. Hertz, explained:

> Chapter 19 [of Numbers] forms the reading for Sabbath Parah, one of the so-called four Extraordinary Sabbaths . . . The reading is to commemorate the purification of the unclean by sprinkling them with the 'water of separation,' so that they may be enabled to bring the Passover sacrifice in a state of purity.[32]

The commentary on the Ezekiel passage in question in this book suggests that the clean water is figurative for "moral purification and inward spiritual renewal."

The need for the "waters of separation" for the cleansing of Israel makes the Sacrifice of the Red Heifer an imperative. Not only for the sake of building the Temple, but for the day Israel turns completely to God to receive a cleansing and a new heart.

The *Miphkad* Altar

There was a specific place on the Mount of Olives where the heifer was sacrificed—directly east of the entrance to the Sanctuary. The place where this rite took place is called the *Miphkad* Altar. There are just a few written references to this altar that must compete with a number of confusing ideas I found on various Internet sites. I have "sorted and sifted" as best I could to present information that can assist our understanding of the sacrificial system and a connection with the Mount of Olives.

We do know there was a bridge from the Temple Mount to the Mount of Olives built of arches upon arches that protected the priest from the possibility of a grave beneath the bridge. This arched bridge is described in the Mishnah (Parah 3, 6) and also by one of the codifiers of Jewish law, Moses Maimonides (1135-1204) as follows:

> A causeway was made from the Temple Mount to the Mount of Olives; it was constructed beneath in the form of arches, with one arch built over the two arches below it, so that underneath the whole there should be some hollow space, for fear of a grave in the depths below. Moreover, <u>beneath the place where she was burnt and the place of immersion, which were on the Mount of Olives</u>, there was a hollow space for fear of a grave in the depths below. And the red heifer, he who should burn her, and all who aided in the burning of her went out from the Temple Mount to the Mount of Olives over this causeway.[33] (Emphasis added.)

There is a hint that the bridge was built and then taken down expressly for the Red Heifer rite. The Mishnah records that the walls on the Temple Mount were high, "with the exception of the eastern wall, so that the [High] Priest who burned the [red] heifer stood on the top of the Mount of Olives and was able to see directly into the entrance of the Sanctuary when the blood was tossed."[34]

There are some clues that the Mount of Olives held special significance as <u>an extension of the Temple</u>. In the Jewish Publication Society's Hebrew Bible is this version of 2 Samuel 15:31-32 where David is fleeing Jerusalem, it reads:

> And David went up by the ascent of the Mount of Olives . . .
> And it came to pass, that when David was come to the top of the ascent, <u>where God was wont to be worshiped</u> . . ."
> (Emphasis added.)

The word *miphkad* in Ezekiel 42:21 is translated as "appointed place" in both the King James Version and in The Jerusalem Bible (published by Koren Publishers in Israel): "Thou shalt take the bullock also of the sin offering, and it shall be burnt in the appointed place of the house, outside the sanctuary."

Miphkad is also found in 2 Samuel 24:9 and 1 Chronicles 21:5, translated as "number" in the section about the census ordered by King David.

Miphkad is discussed at length in Doug Jacoby's scholarly paper on an Internet site, (which you can find at http://www.greatcommission.com/html/TheRedHeiferandtheCrucifixion.html). Jacoby suggests that this word has "etymological reference to counting." The word is found again in Nehemiah 3:31: "over against the gate Miphkad."

Smith's *Bible Dictionary* observes that it was one of the gates of Jerusalem at the time of the rebuilding of the wall following the return from captivity. Smith writes that it was probably not in the wall of Jerusalem proper, but on the north side. But the 1926 *A New Standard Bible Dictionary* has this to say about this obscure gate: "The gate of Hammiphkad—the mustering—(Neh. 3:31), was identical with the old east gate."

We have been taught over the years that the eastern gate on the Temple Mount is the "Golden Gate." It may actually be the "Beautiful Gate" mentioned in Acts 3:2. Apparently, we owe the name *golden* to a mistranslation by Jerome. In an article by James Fleming in the January/February 1983 issue of *Biblical Archaeology Review,* he writes:

> In the earliest Greek New Testament, the word for "beautiful" is *oraia.* When Jerome translated the New Testament into Latin the fourth century, he changed the Greek *oraia* to the similar-sounding Latin *aurea,* rather than the Latin word for "beautiful." So the Latin Vulgate text read "Golden Gate" instead of "Beautiful Gate."

The meaning of *miphkad* is still unclear, whether "appointed place," "appointment," "designated spot," "judgment" or "numbering" (as in a census). I believe the key verse to explain it is in Ezekiel 43:21 where it says, ". . . he shall burn it in the *appointed place* of the house [Temple], without the sanctuary"(emphasis added). It seems credible to me that the *Miphkad* Altar on the Mount of Olives was indeed an extension of the

Temple and was the place where the significant rite of the Red Heifer was carried out, directly east of the Beautiful (Golden) Gate.

I have been told by Rabbi Richman that the probable location of this altar is owned by Muslims and will be one more detail the Lord will have to sort out prior to the rebuilding of His House.

The Wounded Healer

I am indebted to Rabbi Levi Meier, a psychologist at Cedars-Sinai Medical Center in Los Angeles for this closing insight about Numbers 19.

I interviewed Rabbi Meier by phone for a newspaper book review of his book, *Ancient Secrets: Using the Stories of the Bible to Improve Our Everyday Lives.* When I had read what he wrote about the Sacrifice of the Red Heifer, it simply made me weep. I asked Rabbi Meier if it bothered him if a Christian would find such joy in what he wrote. He replied, "Anything I say has to be true for everyone, no matter what culture."

Rabbi Meier points out in his chapter, "The Wounded Healer," that the Sacrifice of the Red Heifer "is a profound paradox—the person who heals becomes wounded by the experience." He discusses how this rite involves mixing ashes and water. The ashes symbolizing death and the water a symbol of life. And then Rabbi Meier wrote something profoundly Messianic to me:

> The priest who administers the rite must himself be a very pure, a very spiritual person. He is required to spend seven days before the ceremony in private retreat, contemplating the cycles of life and death—both the wounds of life and the healing aspects of life. It is essential that he muster all his inner strength for the experience, because, it will transform the person he seeks to cure, as well as himself. <u>One will walk away cured, the other wounded.</u>[35] (Emphasis added.)

It is with the deepest regard for the wisdom and insight of this rabbi, psychologist and family therapist, that I see in Rabbi Meier's words a perfect picture of my *Moshiach,* Jesus of Nazareth. Isaiah's prophecy "he was wounded for our transgressions" echoes down two millennia to a modern-day rabbi who writes about "The Wounded Healer." While this insight would not be accepted by Rabbi Meier, I am deeply indebted to him for it nonetheless.

1. *The Zohar,* translated by Maurice Simon and Dr. Paul P. Levertoff, The Soncino Press, London, 1984, Vol. 4, page 373.

2. *Midrash Rabbah,* Numbers Vol. II, Soncino Press, 1983, page 754.

3. C.G. Montefiore & H. Loewe, *A Rabbinic Anthology,* Schocken Books, New York, 1974, page 150.

4. Rabbi Chaim Richman, *The Mystery of the Red Heifer: Divine Promise of Purity,* Jerusalem, 1997, page 9.

5. James Bentley, *The Epistle of Barnabus* as cited in *Secrets of Mount Sinai: The Story of the World's Oldest Bible—Codex Sinaiticus,* Doubleday & Company, Inc., Garden City, New York, 1986, page 224.

6. C.H. Mackintosh, *Genesis to Deuteronomy: Notes on the Pentateuch,* originally published as individual volumes, 1880-1882; published in one volume, Loizeaux Brothers, Inc., New Jersey, 1972, page 546.

7. Adam Clarke, *The Old Testament with a Commentary and Critical Notes,* Vol. 1, G. Lane & P.P. Sanford, New York, 1843, page 678.

8. Josephus, *The Wars of the Jews,* translated by William Whiston, Kregel Publications, 1960, Book Six, page 582.

9. R.C. Sproul, *The Last Days According to Jesus,* Baker Books, Michigan, 1999, page 122.

10. Baruch A. Levine, *Numbers 1-20: A New Translation with Introduction and Commentary,* The Anchor Bible, Doubleday, 1993, page 460.

11. *The Zohar,* translated by Maurice Simon and Dr. Paul P. Levertoff, The Soncino Press, London, 1984, Vol. II, page 360.

12. C.F. Keil and F. Delitzch, *Commentary on the Old Testament in Ten Volumes,* William B. Eerdmans Publishing Company, 1985, Vol. 1, page 122.

13. Talmud, Ta'anit 20b .

14. Rabbi Solomon ben Isaac (acronym "Rashi") as cited in *Rashi,* Chaim Pearl, Grove Press, New York, 1988, page 46.

15. John Morison, as quoted in *The Treasury of David,* C.H. Spurgeon, Hendrickson Publishers, n.d., Vol. I, page 416.

16. Grant R. Jeffrey, *The Signature of God,* Frontier Research Publications, Toronto, 1996, page 153.

17. Herbert Lockyer, *All the Messianic Prophecies of the Bible,* Zondervan Publishing House, 1973, Grand Rapids, Michigan, page 371.

18. Samuel Sandmel, *We Jews and Jesus,* New York Oxford University Press, 1965, page 12.

19. D.L. Higginbotham, *Color in Scripture,* Truth for Today Bible Fellowship, Lafayette, Indiana, 1992, page 10.

20. Alfred Edersheim, *The Temple: Its Ministry and Services,* Wm. B. Eerdman's Publishing Company, 1987, page 55.

21. Richard Booker, *The Miracle of the Scarlet Thread,* Destiny Image Publishers, 1981, preface.

22. E.W. Bullinger, *The Book of Job: A New Translation,* Kregel Publications, 1990, page page ix.

23. Baruch Levine, *Numbers 1-20,* The Anchor Bible, Doubleday, 1993, page 462.

24. Rabbi Chaim Richman, *The Mystery of the Red Heifer: Divine Promise of Purity,* Jerusalem, 1997, page 49.

25. Henry W. Soltau, *The Tabernacle: The Priesthood and the Offering,* (originally published c. 1867) Kregel Publications, 1972, pages 113-115.

26. E.W. Bullinger, *Number in Scripture,* Kregel Publications, 1967, page 161.

27. Adam Clarke, *The Old Testament with a Commentary and Critical Notes,* Vol. 1, G. Lane & P.P. Sanford, New York, 1843, pages 266-267.

28. Marvin R. Vincent, D.D., *Word Studies in the New Testament,* Hendrickson Publishers, originally published 1886, Vol. II, page 183.

29. Ibid.

30. Rabbi Yisrael Ariel, translated and adapted by Chaim Richman, *The Odyssey of the Third Temple,* G. Israel Publications & Productions Ltd./The Temple Institute, Jerusalem, Av 5753, page 47.

31. Alfred Edersheim, *The Temple: Its Ministry and Service,* Wm. B. Eerdman's Publishing Company, 1987, page 281.

32. *Pentateuch and Haftorahs,* edited by Dr. J.H. Hertz, Soncino Press, London, 1962, page 655.

33. Moses Maimonides, *The Code of Maimonides, Book Ten: The Book of Cleanness,* translated by Herbert Danby, Yale University Press, 1954, page 103.

34. *Mishnayoth,* Judaica Press, Ltd., Gateshead, England, 1983, Vol. 5, *Middoth,* pages 511-512.

35. Rabbi Levi Meier, *Ancient Secrets: Using the Stories of the Bible to Improve Our Everyday Lives,* Villard Books, 1996, page 183.

Chapter Three

The Coming Temple in Jerusalem

For more than 2,000 years no prophet has arisen in our midst who announces to us G-d's Word and His decisions. But nevertheless, all our longing, hoping and waiting are concentrated upon the unforgettable ruin of the Temple in Jerusalem, so that from there a new light would illuminate the world and bring back the vanished happiness of mankind, and to the nations the lost peace.

— Bavarian Rabbi Elchanan Pinchas Moshe Chaim
(called Reb Hile Wechsler) 1843-1894.[1]

Before the Jews can rebuild the Temple, they must be purified with the Ashes of the Red Heifer. But are we Christians sure that prophecy indeed foretells a Temple? Is a Temple in Jerusalem so necessary for Endtime events to play out that this rare red calf must be sacrificed?

I can't help but believe that when the Bible speaks—the debate is over! That's why I think Chuck Missler had the last word when he said there WILL be a Temple in Jerusalem because it is discussed in both the Old and New Testament. In the book he co-authored with Don Stewart, *The Coming Temple*, Missler discusses the fact that there are three passages in the Old Testament that speak of the defiling of a future temple. None of them have been literally fulfilled:

And he shall confirm the covenant with many for one week: and in the midst of the week he shall cause the sacrifice and the oblation to cease and for the overshadowing of abominations he shall make it desolate, even until the consumption, and that determined shall be poured upon the desolate. Daniel 9:27

And arms [forces] shall stand on his part, and they shall pollute the <u>sanctuary</u> of strength, and shall take away the daily sacrifice, and they shall place the abomination that maketh desolate. Daniel 11:31

And from the time that the daily sacrifice shall be taken away, and the abomination that maketh desolate set up, there shall be a thousand two hundred and ninety days. Daniel 12:11. (Emphasis added.)

Missler notes that "Jesus spoke of this prophecy being still future to His time (Matthew 24:15)." These aren't the only verses that foretell a temple in the New Testament—2 Thessalonians 2:3,4 tell about the son of perdition who opposes and exalts himself above God and "sitteth in the temple of God, shewing himself that he is God." Missler says that the word translated as "Temple" is not the generic word for the Temple and its buildings but *naos* the "Sanctuary," or the Holy of Holies.[2]

And in the final scriptural reference, John wrote in Revelation 11:1,2 about measuring the temple of God and leaving out the outer court "for it has been given to the Gentiles." This scripture suggests that the size of the Temple will not need to be as large as Herod's Temple, because apparently the area of the outer court will still be held by Gentiles (the Muslims?).

Article 8 of the 1948 armistice agreement (between Israel and the Arab nations that attacked it following the declaration of Israel's statehood) guaranteed Israelis the right to worship at the Western Wall, the only remnant of the Temple that survived the Roman destruction. For 19 long years the Jews were denied this right. I have a photo of a group of Jews each wrapped in a prayer shawl (*tallith*) praying from the roof of the King David Hotel toward the Western Wall. This was the closest they were allowed. Ezekiel 36:2 seems to foretell this very fact: ". . . the enemy hath said against you, Aha, even the ancient high places are ours in possession." No wonder the battle-weary soldiers and paratroopers who swept into East Jerusalem in June of 1967 could only bow their heads and weep against those ancient Herodian stones of the Western Wall. When Jews place such emphasis on the mere outer wall of the Temple, their determination to rebuild the Temple is all the more understandable.

But the actual building of this Temple encounters an insurmountable obstacle—the fact that Muslims control the Temple Mount in Jerusalem. In an effort to show the peaceful intent of Israel, the secular Israeli leader Moshe Dayan turned control back to the Muslim Waqf after Israel regained East Jerusalem in the Six Day War. Religious Jews have mourned that decision ever since, for it certainly did not ease Muslim hatred of the Jews and it effectively denied Jews access to their holiest place.

The Muslim's venerated shrine, the Dome of the Rock, is the focus of many Jewish Temple hopes, for it sits in a prominent place atop the Temple Mount. Unfortunately, in the face of indisputable historical and archaeological evidence, the Muslims continue to deny there ever was a Temple in Jerusalem, as if that could prevent a Third Temple.

The Jerusalem Post recently reported a most telling fact: The Post's January 26, 2001 edition noted that a 1930 booklet about the Temple Mount stated it is "beyond dispute" that this site is identified with Solomon's Temple. The English-language booklet was published by the Supreme Moslem Council and titled *A brief Guide to al-Haram al-Sharif.* The Jerusalem Post obtained a copy and quoted the following from it:

> The site is one of the oldest in the world. Its sanctity dates from the earliest times. Its identity with the site of Solomon's Temple is beyond dispute. This, too, is the spot, according to universal belief, on which David built there

an altar unto the Lord, and offered burnt offerings and peace offerings.

My 1960 edition of this booklet (printed by the Industrial Islamic Orphanage Press, Jerusalem) is titled *A Brief Guide to The Dome of the Rock and Al-Haram Al-Sharif.* The booklet was expanded from its original nine pages to 98. But any connection to the site of Solomon's Temple was obliterated. The closest the author or authors would come to admitting an earlier sanctity is found on page 10, where it is stated: "The decision to built (sic) the new sanctuary over the Rock was quite natural because of its many associations." Historical associations perhaps?

The 1930 section discussing the substructure of the Dome of the Rock was left out of the 1960 version. The earlier guide had noted that "little is known for certain about the early history of the chamber itself. It dates probably as far back at the construction of Solomon's Temple. . . According to Josephus, it was in existence and was used as a place of refuge by the Jews at the time of the conquest of Jerusalem by Titus in the year 70 A.D."

The Post concluded its article by quoting Palestinian Authority Mufti Ikrima Sabri who was interviewed the same week by the German *Die Welt* and said, "There is not [even] the smallest indication of the existence of a Jewish temple on this place in the past. In the whole city, there is not even a single stone indicating Jewish history."

In a desperate bid to shore up his re-election hopes in the waning days of January 2001, Prime Minister Ehud Barak finally ordered police to put a halt to the excavation work of the Waqf and the Israeli Islamic Movement. For nearly a year, *Biblical Archaeology Review* has lobbied Israeli officials to halt the bulldozing that surely is destroying any Jewish presence on the Temple Mount.

Even if Muslims manage to erase any current archaeological suggestion of Jewish presence on the Temple Mount, how can they explain away the numerous archaeological finds safely sequestered in museums around the world? No one but these Muslims doubts the validity of Solomon's and Herod's Temples in antiquity.

Where Should the Temple Be Built?

There are three main theories about exactly where the Temple was located on the Temple Mount. Israeli archaeologist Dan Bahat, former chief archaeologist for the Jerusalem region, marshals compelling evidence that the Temple stood where the Dome of the Rock is now. Chuck Missler writes

Model of Herod's Temple, Holyland Hotel, Jerusalem

that Bahat has reviewed the archaeological history of the Temple Mount area with particular reference to the Dome of the Rock. Following the 1993 Temple Conference he hosted in Jerusalem, Missler reported this about Bahat's belief of where the Temple stood:

> The traditional site of the Temple is where there is presently a Moslem shrine known as the Dome of the Rock. Ostensibly built by the Moslems to overlay the location of the original Jewish Temple(s), most rabbis in Israel today associate the original Temple location with this site. Recent journal articles still support this view.

Indeed, two of the most prominent temple groups, The Temple Mount and Land of Israel Faithful Movement and the Temple Institute, also firmly declare that the Temple must be built on the site of the Dome of the Rock. How can this possibly happen knowing the Muslim fervor for the golden dome? At the 1992 Temple Conference in Jerusalem, Rabbi Chaim Richman answered that question by saying, "We leave that up to G-d more or less or the government of Israel, whichever comes first."

And during a speaking tour of the U.S. in June 1998, Gershon Saloman, head of Temple Mount Faithful, said that Israel must dismantle the Dome of the Rock "stone-by-stone, put it in an envelope and mail it to Mecca." One of the Temple Mount Faithful brochures states this a little more diplomatically: "It has been suggested that [the Dome of the Rock and the al-Aqsa mosque] be removed, transferred to and rebuilt at Mecca." The actual transferral of the buildings would not be an impossible task. Think of the two colossal temples of Ramses II that were moved to Abu Simbel during the construction of the Aswan Dam in Egypt. However, convincing Islam to move its Jerusalem shrines is another matter altogether.

Tel Aviv architect Tuvia Sagiv suggests an alternative Temple location: that the Temple site was south of the Dome of the Rock, with the Holy of Holies located approximately where the Al-Kas washing fountain is, between the Dome of the Rock and the Al Aqsa Mosque. Using the locations of water sources and accounts about the height of certain walls from the Antonio Fortress, Sagiv believes he can prove the Temple was sited to the south of the Dome of the Rock.

Agrippa's View

Chuck Missler writes the following description about Sagiv's theory:

> Josephus, in *The Jewish Wars*, describes that Agrippa could look out from the Hasmonean Palace and view the sacrifices at the Azara, at the altar. This incensed the Jews who then built a wall in order to block out the view. Roman solders, patrolling the western threshold, were thus unable to view the Azara, and demanded that the wall be demolished. The Jews objected, and even obtained the consent of Emperor Nero to leave the wall in place.

If the Temple was at the location of the Dome of the Rock, the Hasmonean Palace would have required a height of 75 meters to view into the Azara. There never was a building of such a height in Jerusalem. This implies a lower, more southernly location.

The Water Aqueduct

Missler continues with Sagiv's findings on an ancient water aquaduct:

The water canals that supplied Jerusalem began in the area of the Hebron mountains, passed through Solomon's Pools, and flowed to Jerusalem. The lowest canal reached the Temple Mount through the Jewish Quarter and the Wilson Bridge. According to the ancient authorities, the water conduit supplied water to the High Priests' mikva (ritual bath) located above the Water Gate, and it also supplied water for the rinsing of the blood off the Azara.

A survey of the level of the aqueduct reveals that if the Temple was at the Dome of the Rock, the aqueduct would be over 20 meters too low to serve either the Azara or the Water Gate. From this survey, it appears that the Temple must have been 20 meters lower and, thus, to the south.[3]

Missler also notes that Sagiv has infrared thermographic scans that also seem to support the southern view.[4]

The Northern Location

Although I must admit that Sagiv's research is intriguing, the third theory about the Temple's location has always seemed the most plausible to me. This theory, which places the Temple site north of the Dome of the Rock, will necessitate a quick look at history.

The total area of the Temple Mount (called *Haram es-Sharif* or Noble Sanctuary in Arabic) is approximately 34 acres. This ground is sacred to Jews, Muslims and Christians and was the foundation for Solomon's Temple (demolished in 587 B.C.) and the temple Herod reconstructed. All but Herod's Western Wall was destroyed by the Romans in 70 A.D. Various conquerors built houses of worship on the mount, which were demolished and built over by the next conqueror.

The rock that Abraham was to sacrifice his son Isaac upon supposedly lies under the Dome of the Rock, completed in 691 A.D. The Qu'ran says Mohammed visited the "furthermost place" (*masjad al-Aqsa*) and rose to heaven, leaving his footprint (or his horse's print, the stories differ) in the rough rock mass.

This same rock is venerated by many Orthodox Jews as *Even Shitiyah*, the "Foundation Stone" that the Ark of the Covenant was placed upon in the Holy of Holies. The Holy of Holies was so sacred that only the High Priest could enter, and then only on one day of the year, on Yom Kippur (The Day of Atonement). To this day, Orthodox rabbis prohibit Jews from stepping on the Temple Mount lest they accidentally tread upon the holy place. But religious Jews who feel certain of the location of the Holy of Holies have continued quiet observations on the Temple Mount. (And *quiet observations* indeed describe any activity on the Temple Mount. Just let your lips move in prayer, (let alone kneel!), and you will be immediately escorted off the Temple Mount by Waqf police.)

Asher Kaufman's Northern Theory

Hebrew University professor Asher Kaufman believes that the rock sacred to Muslims is *not* the Foundation Stone and, in fact, lies 330 meters from where the ancient Jewish temple stood.

In an article published in the March/April 1983 issue of *Biblical Archaeology Review* (BAR), Kaufman reported the results of almost 20 years of research on the Temple Mount centered around a small cupola on the northwestern corner of the temple platform. Called *Qubbat el-Arwah*

(Dome of the Spirits) and *Qubbat el-Alouah* (Dome of the Tablets), the cupola covers a section of bedrock that is just one meter lower than the bedrock under the Dome of the Rock. Kaufman believes the Arab names commemorate the belief that the Spirit of God dwelt above the Ark of the Covenant (Dome of the Spirits) and that the Ark contained the Ten Commandments written on stone tablets (the Dome of the Tablets).

Dr. Asher Kaufman at the Temple Conference in Jerusalem

Kaufman produces literary evidence from the *Mishnah* (oral tradition codified about 200 A.D.) and the *Tosefta* (addition or commentary on the Talmud, which is itself, commentary on the Mishnah) from that same period, that show the temple's dimensions would prohibit placement over the Dome of the Rock. "When the Temple plan is laid out on the Temple Mount according to this [Dome of the Rock] location of the Holy of Holies, there is very little room between the eastern wall of the Temple and the eastern outer wall of the Temple Mount," writes Kaufman.

Professor Kaufman provides more than tradition to prove his point. He explains that a British expedition in 1864-65 mapped 20 underground cisterns beneath the Temple platform which can be identified with ancient temple documents. In this issue of BAR he writes: "My comprehensive recording and mapping of the available archaeological evidence above ground were the first to be conducted systematically and scientifically. The finds above ground included rock cuttings, rows of stones, wall remains and sections of pavement, as well as artifacts such as mosaic cubes, glass fragments and potsherds."

One of the "rows of stones" was discovered as the result of a fire set in the al-Aqsa Mosque in 1969 by an Australian tourist who was later found mentally ill. To improve fire-fighting capabilities on the mount, a pit was dug by a bulldozer by the Muslim Council. On November 7, 1970 Dr. Ze'ev Yeivin of the Israel Department of Antiquities and Museums was called to the Mount to inspect an ancient wall that had been uncovered. He wrote in a report that the carefully chiseled stones "were reminiscent of Herodian masonry. It is quite possible that we have here a part of Herodian building on the Temple Mount." Muslim authorities demolished the wall and removed the stones. No further archaeological work has been allowed.

Kaufman reviewed the report in 1978 and found it confirmed his previous surveys. He concluded: "The wall Yeivin had seen was the foundation of the eastern wall of the Second Temple compound itself." Kaufman then laid out the plan of the temple over the bedrock of the Dome of the Spirits and found that in a direct line east, this temple plan lines up exactly with the eastern gate, called the Golden Gate, of Jerusalem's wall. The current eastern gate is built upon an earlier, ancient gate.[5]

It is known that the High Priest sprinkled the Red Heifer's blood toward the Sanctuary of the Temple, which he could observe through the eastern gate as he stood on the Mount of Olives. Mishnah Middoth 2,4 reads: "All the walls that were there [on the Temple Mount] were high, with the exception of the eastern wall, so that the [High] Priest who burned the [red] heifer stood on the top of the Mount of Olives and was able to see directly into the entrance of the Sanctuary when the blood was tossed."

Biblical researcher and author Hal Lindsey wrote this regarding Kaufman's theory:

> I believe that Dr. Kaufman's dedicated and tireless inves-
> tigation has provided the world with a priceless discovery.
>
> I also believe that this discovery has accelerated the
> countdown to the events that will bring the Messiah Jesus
> back to earth. The reason for this belief is that the
> predicted Third Temple can now be built without
> disturbing the Dome of the Rock. As shown on the chart

[page 74 of Lindsey's *A Prophetical Walk Through the Holy Land*], the Temple and its immediate guard wall could be rebuilt and still be twenty-six meters away from the Dome of the Rock.

Revelation chapter 11 indicates this very situation: "I was given a reed like a measuring rod and was told, 'Go and measure the temple of God and the altar, and count the worshipers there. But exclude THE OUTER COURT; do not measure it, because it has been given to the GENTILES. They will trample on the holy city for 42 months.'" (Revelation 11:1, 2, NIV, emphasis added by Lindsey).

The outer court, which includes the area where the Dome of the Rock is situated, was given to the Gentiles. So this prophecy accurately reflects the situation that is present today.[6]

With much evidence suggesting that the Dome of the Rock is not the correct site for the temple, why is it the favored location among Orthodox Jews? What if the Temple is rebuilt on the wrong location? Several biblical commentators suggest that since Christians believe this is a Temple built to be desecrated by the Antichrist, perhaps it is God's will that this temple be built over the wrong bedrock on the mount. And this may be one of the instances of scripture where we won't know—until it actually happens before our very eyes—exactly how God will fulfill it.

Jeremy Boren and Margaret Murphy visit Jerusalem to see the site that Asher Kaufman believes is the true location of the Holy of Holies of Herod's Temple

Whatever the controversies about the location of the Temple, a Temple will be built. And recent activities in Jerusalem show how close we are to seeing this prophetic structure built.

The Temple Institute

Rabbi Chaim Richman, has been with the Temple Institute for many years and also served as the director of "Canaan Land Restoration of Israel," (the name of the organization formed to take Rev. Lott's red Angus cattle to Israel, now called "Lott's Cattle"). Rabbi Richman often says, "there must be a stirring below before there is a stirring above," when he wants to remind his audiences that God will not move to help us unless we make a move first. That might help Christians understand why Orthodox Jews have been preparing for the coming Temple even though right now it seems utterly impossible to build it.

The Temple Institute is a must-see in the Jewish Quarter of Jerusalem near the Western Wall. The organization was founded by Rabbi Israel Ariel who was one of the first paratroopers to reach the Western Wall in 1967. In *The Odyssey of the Third Temple* by Rabbi Ariel, translated and adapted by Rabbi Richman, it is written: "The Temple Institute in Jerusalem is a waystation, a sort of 'Temple-in-Waiting' which was founded in order to prepare as best as possible for the building of the Holy Temple. For the conclusion of everything we have studied so far is that we arise and act." Rabbi Ariel writes of the faith-affirming words of the Children of Israel when given the Ten Commandments: "We shall do and we shall obey." He concludes:

> "The power of these words is that Israel declared 'we will do' everything that is in our power to do. Even if everything is not perfectly understood, we will still give our utmost to 'do'—and only as things begin to develop can we expect to 'obey' on an intellectual level . . . to understand. With God's help we will complete the task, even though it does not always seem humanly possible."[7]

The Temple Institute has crafted more than 70 of the 93 vessels needed for temple worship. The Mishnah (Tamid 3,4) says: "They went into the Chamber of Utensils and brought forth (thence) ninety-three vessels of silver and vessels of gold." That may seem like a lot of vessels and implements, but the Temple Service was a seven-day-a-week operation that involved tending the lights of the Temple, preparing the incense and burnt offerings daily.

Rabbi Richman holds the gold mizrach recreated by the Temple Institute to hold the blood of the sacrifices.

And think of the number of Passover pilgrims who swelled the population of Jerusalem each year, each family with a lamb to be slain. Can you begin to imagine the orchestration of thousands of lambs killed and their blood taken to the great altar of the Temple to be sprinkled? Think of organizing it!

The biblical scholar Alfred Edersheim has written extensively about this immense task:

> "How large the number of worshipers was, may be gathered from Josephus, who records that, when Cestius requested the high priest to make a census, in order to convince Nero of the importance of Jerusalem and of the Jewish nation, the number of lambs slain was found to be 265,500, which, at the lowest computation of ten persons to every sacrificial lamb, would give a population of 2,565,000 or as Josephus himself puts it, 2,700,200 persons, while on an earlier occasion (A.D. 65) he computes the number present at not fewer than three millions."[8]

Jewish scholar Eliyahu Kitov quotes Maimonides who said that the slaughtering of the Pesach (Passover) offering was done in three groups:

"When the first group had filled the courtyard to capacity, the doors were closed and the slaughter of the animals began. Throughout the slaughtering and the offering up, the Levites would sing the Hallel. If the first group of people had not yet finished their tasks, the Levites would repeat the Hallel a second time and even a third time if necessary, although this never happened." (Rambam Hilchot Korban Pesach).

Then Kitov notes:

"The cohanim [priests] stood row after row with dishes of silver and dishes of gold in their hands. The whole of one row had silver dishes and the whole of another row had golden ones and they remained separate so that it would appear even more beautiful. These vessels were wide at the top and pointed at the bottom so that they could not be put down on the ground, for the blood in them might congeal and be unsuitable to sprinkle on the altar.

When the animal had been slaughtered, the cohen would receive the blood in the vessels and hand it on to his fellow and he to the next one so that many people should have a share in the mitzvah [good deed]. When it reached the cohen who was nearest to the altar he would toss it in one swift motion, against the base. As he received a full vessel, with one hand, he would pass an empty one to his fellow with the other hand."[9]

Kitov also lists an incredible eyewitness description of the ceremony of the Pesach sacrifice by a Roman soldier stationed in Jerusalem shortly before the destruction of the Second Temple:

> When the beginning of the month, which they call Nisan, arrives, couriers and messengers are sent out by order of the king and the judges, to all the area surrounding Jerusalem that whosoever possesses sheep and cattle should hurry to bring them to the capital so that there be a sufficient supply for the pilgrims, both for their sacrifices and for their food . . . All owners of cattle would hurry to obey and, on the way to Jerusalem they would bring their herds through a river to cleanse them of any dirt. When they reach the mountains round Jerusalem, they are so numerous that the grass cannot be seen. It appears to have become completely white because of the many sheep there.

The soldier describes the cohenim standing in rows with the gold and silver mizrakim:

> "The cohen at the head of each row receives a spoon [vessel] of blood from the slaughtered animal and passes it to his neighbor until it reaches the altar. The one standing nearest the altar would send back the spoon empty and this would be passed from hand to hand until it reached the other end of the row. This was done in such a way that each cohen received a full vessel with one hand and an empty one with the other. There was no delay in this procedure. The men were so nimble that it seemed as if the vessels were flying like arrows from the bow of a trained marksman. They used to practice this for thirty

days before the required time so that there should be no mistake and they would know their task perfectly."[10]

The Temple Institute has on display a golden *mizrak* of exquisite craftsmanship that is wide at the top and pointed at the bottom as described above. This vessel will be used to catch the blood of a sacrifice and then be carried to the altar of the Temple.

We can now understand that many *mizrakim* will be needed when observant Jews bring their Pesach sacrifice to Jerusalem. In *The Odyssey of the Third Temple*, Rabbi Ariel lists the number of implements that will be needed just to carry out sacrifices on the Burnt-Offering Altar:

Utensils for the Burnt-Offering Altar
4 Stoking Shovels
4 Pans
10 Containment Vessels
7 Trays
5 Forks
4 Ash-Carts

The Temple Institute must prepare not only these vessels but priests' clothing, musical instruments for the Levites, the gold Menorah, the Shewbread Table, the Incense Altar, even the Breastplate of the High Priest.

At the Temple Institute you can see the loom where garments for the priests are woven with 6 threads as specified in scripture. Gold-plated *shofarot* (ram's horns) are on display along with silver trumpets and harps made by the House of Harrari. Artisans have crafted a magnificent gold flask for the Festival of the Water Libation and a silver decanter for the twice-daily wine libation to be poured upon the altar. A large copper laver and stand is ready for the washing of priests' hands and feet. The spices and oils needed for the incense have been identified and gathered. The High Priest's gold crown (which is not worn on his head but across his forehead) is awaiting use, with "Holy to the Lord" written in beautiful Hebrew script. The lottery box is complete with the two lots: one for the Lord and one for *Azazel* to determine which goat goes into the wilderness on Yom Kippur or the Day of Atonement.

In one of Rabbi Richman's e-mail newsletters dated February 20, 2000, he announced some special news: "It is a cause of great joy for us to report that as part of its ongoing program to restore the vessels of the Holy Temple, the Temple Institute has recently completed the golden Table for the Showbread, ready to stand with the twelve loaves of special bread, one representing each tribe of Israel, within the hallowed Sanctuary of the Holy Temple. Thus, the Institute has now completed the three major, central vessels which stand within the holy area of the Temple—the Menorah, the Incense Altar, and the Table."

There is also an incredible bookstore at the Temple Institute with reference material regarding the Temple and its services. No trip to Jerusalem is complete without touring the breathtaking exhibits of the Temple Institute.

It is stunning to those who believe in prophecy to hear of the intense research about the location of the Temple and the fact that there is an organization such as the Temple Institute creating the vestments and implements needed for Temple worship. As you ponder Christ's direction to watch for the prophetic "fig leaves" that signal His return, you find that the entire fig tree is in bloom! Consider the following developments that occurred in 1997 and 1998 alone:

The Holy Half-Shekel Temple Tax

In November of 1997, I had the great honor of arranging the visit to Salt Lake City of Rabbi Chaim Richman and Rev. Clyde Lott. These two men of God came to share their story of the Mississippi Red Heifer. As a thank-you gift, Rabbi Richman presented me with a small envelope that touched my heart: inside was a pure silver ceremonial Holy Half-Shekel. I keep this beautiful coin tucked in my Bible. It comes in a small presentation envelope with a certificate noting that the Holy Half-Shekel was struck in Jerusalem and exceeds in purity and weight, the *Halachah* or legal requirements of Exodus 30:11-16 where the Children of Israel were commanded to donate a half-shekel yearly for the upkeep of the Tabernacle and ultimately, the Temple in Jerusalem.

An advertisement from the Israeli company *Beged Ivri* that ran in a 1997 International Jerusalem Post depicted the coin with the following description:

> Obverse: The Prophetic ten stringed lyre of the Third Temple era. . . As we have no custom of dating our coinage by foreign calendars, nor even from Creation, we took the example of our predecessors and dated our ceremonial coin from the Liberation of the Land of Israel. This year's coin, to be given on Purim of 1998, will open the 50th Year celebration of the State of Israel.
>
> Reverse: A pair of hands joining together in the manner of the Priestly Blessing, offering a Half-Shekel towards Heaven. The Half-Shekel ascends as a 'Coin of Fire' skyward. The hands symbolize the Temple Service, which is budgeted from the *Trumath Haliskhah* (Appropriations), from the Half-Shekels donated each year, and suggests the coming together of opposites: the left and the right, the religious and the secular, the fundamentalists and the modernizers, each but a half, needing the 'other' to complete themselves.

For almost two thousand years no Jew could fulfill the commandment of Deuteronomy 30 to pay his Temple Tax. Because the pure silver coin (acceptable for donation to the Temple) has been reintroduced, we are blessed to have witnessed yet one more restoration, moving the world closer to the Holy Temple in Jerusalem and the Time of Redemption.

A Cohen by Any Other Name is a
"Patrilineal YAP, DYS19B Haplotype?"

When the Jews returned from the Babylonian captivity, there were problems restoring Temple Service. First, many obstacles had to be overcome to rebuild the Temple and then the Cohanim had to prove their genealogy. (Note: You will see the Hebrew word for 'priest' spelled both '*Cohen*' and '*Kohen.*')

Ezra 2:59 describes the problem some would-be priests encountered when they returned to Jerusalem: "And these were they which went up from Tel-Melah, Tel-Harsa, Cherub, Addan and Immer: but they could not shew their father's house, and their seed, whether they were of Israel."

The verses that follow tell of the men who could not prove they were of Israel. Verses 62-63 explain: "These sought after their register among those that were reckoned by genealogy, but they were not found: therefore were they, as polluted, put from the priesthood. And the Tirshatha [Nehemiah's Persian title, cf. Nehemiah 8:9] said unto them, that they should not eat of the most holy things, till there stood up a priest with Urim and Thummim." Because these men had no proof that they were of the priestly lineage, they were barred from serving as priests.

Today the Jews are back in the land after an almost two-thousand-year dispersal. And some of them have family traditions of being Cohens. How will they prove their lineage?

The late biblical scholar Joachim Jeremias wrote: "There was in the Temple at Jerusalem a kind of archive in which the genealogies of the priesthood were kept."[11] Jeremias documents this from *Siphre Num. Korah* 116 on 18:7.

Unfortunately, those precious genealogical records were destroyed in 70 A.D. by the Romans when they set the Temple on fire and dismantled the massive building stone-by-stone..

No Jew who survived to watch the Temple and its records burn could have dreamed what God had arranged to come forth in these last days when the rebuilding is beginning! What if God's foreknowledge had allowed for the "printing" of lineage in an indestructible manner? No matter what Satan ever managed to do to block God's plans, the solution was created before the problem! You will discover below that God's imprint is more astounding than you could have ever imagined!

Biblical researcher and teacher Grant R. Jeffrey wrote the following article for the website *The Y Files* (www.yfiles.com):

> A newspaper report from Jerusalem dated January 3, 1997 indicates that scientists have found a unique genetic chromosome linking Jews of the priestly tribe (Kohanim) worldwide. The researchers found these Jewish Kohanim, whether from the Ashkenazi (European) or the Sephardi (Spanish and Middle Eastern) branches share a variation of the Y chromosome. This is a very strong evidence that these individuals are descendants of one man, Aaron the High Priest, who lived 3,500 years ago. Professor Karl Skorecki, a senior nephrologist (blood specialist) at Rambam Hospital in Haifa is the head of molecular medicine at Israel's Technion medical school. He and his colleagues published their findings in *Nature*, a British science journal.
>
> The scientists obtained genetic samples from the insides of the cheeks of unrelated Jewish men who lived in three nations. They asked if they were Kohanim, related to the priestly tribe. The genetic phenotypes of 188 Jews who believed they were descended from the Kohanim were different genetically from those Jews in the sample who were not Kohanim. The researchers found a preponderance of the YAP, DYS19B haplotype in the priestly Kohanim. This Y chromosome is carried only by men and is passed down father to son patrilineally. Mitochondrial DNA, on the other hand, is transmitted by the mother's X chromosome. Professor Skorecki explained

that it was impressive how the characteristic Y chromosome was passed down the generations despite centuries of assimilation over the last two thousand years. Professor Skorecki did not choose Kohanim based on their names (Cohen, Rappaport or Shapiro, etc.). Rather, they asked if their family tradition claimed they were Kohanim.

The professor himself is a Kohen. He noticed another Kohen in a synagogue and wondered if they could be genetically linked since the Bible claimed they were all descended from Aaron. "I wanted to know if it were possible to find a genetic connection." It is estimated that approximately 5 percent (350,000 men) of the 7 million male Jews worldwide are descended from the priestly tribe. The priests led Israel in its worship in the Temple and Tabernacle from the time of Aaron. . . Since the Roman army burned the Temple in A.D. 70 the Kohanim priesthood required its members to keep ritually pure by not touching a corpse or marrying a divorcee.[12]

Because there is no prophet in Israel with a Urim and Thummim (oracle worn by the High Priest in or on his jeweled breastplate, Numbers 27:21) who can declare from God who is of the lineage to be a priest, God has supernaturally engineered proof in the very life code of each and every Cohen. Satan may rage among the nations, but God is always one step ahead.

Even before this DNA miracle was discovered, young priests were in training in Jerusalem. In the Oct. 16, 1989 Time magazine, an article stated: "Two Talmudic schools located near the Western (Wailing) Wall are teaching nearly 200 students the elaborate details of the Temple service. Other groups are researching family lines of Jewish priests who alone may conduct sacrifices." Three times a day these young priests-in-training pray these words: "May it be Thy will that the Temple be speedily rebuilt in our days." And then they learn how to serve in that Temple!

The Blue "Fig Leaf"—*Tekhelet*

For centuries, Jews have mourned the loss of knowing how to make the *tekhelet* dye for the blue thread in the fringe on prayer shawls and the religious garment called a *tallit katan*, worn during waking hours by Orthodox men. The prayer book of Rabbi Nachman of Bratslav has this plea to the Lord: "Have mercy on us and rebuild Your city speedily in our days, and return us to peace, to our holy land, and let us merit the return and revelation of the *Hilazon* [the marine animal from which the dye comes], that we may be privileged to fulfill the commandment of tekhelet in *tsitsit* (the Hebrew word for fringe)."

In the Midrash Rabbah it says, ". . .it is a religious duty to get white wool and a blue thread and make the fringes. When does this rule apply? When the thread is real blue. Now, however, we possess only white, for the blue has been (divinely) hidden."[13]

The commandment is:

> Speak unto the children of Israel, and bid them that they make them fringes in the borders of their garments throughout the generations, and that they put upon the fringe of the borders a ribband of blue: And it shall be unto you for a fringe, that ye may look upon it, and remember all the commandments of the Lord, and do them; and that you seek not after your heart and your own eyes, after which ye use to go a whoring: That ye may remember, and do all my commandments, and be holy unto your God. Numbers 15:37-40.

Biblical scholar Jacob Milgrom makes an interesting conjecture that I believe shows an Old Testament shadowing of the New Testament idea that all men could become priests before God:

The Bible contains a general prohibition against cloth that combines wool and linen, which is referred to by the untranslatable term *sha'atnez* (Deuternomy 22:12; cf. Leviticus 19:19). Some of the early commentaries (for example Targum Pseudo-Jonathan on Deuteronomy 22:12), however, indicate that *sha'atnez*—this combination of wood and linen—was sanctioned and even required in priestly garments. And this rabbinic suggestion has now been confirmed archaeologically. Tassels dating to the Bar Kokhba period (c. 135 A.D.) were found in the Dead Sea caves. These tassels were made of white cords of linen and blue cords of wool, demonstrating that the rabbinic teaching was not speculative abstraction but actual practice.

Thus, the reason for the prohibition against *sha'atnez*—cloth or garments combining wool and linen is clear: it would resemble some of the priestly garments made from a blend of linen and wool (e.g., Exodus 28:6; 39:29; Mishna Kelayim 9:1). Therefore, the combination of wool and linen (*sha'atnez*) is forbidden to the lay Israelite because it is a holy mixture and reserved exclusively for the sanctuary (e.g., Exodus 26:1) and the priests.

By using the combination of wool and linen in the tassel, the ordinary Israelite was, however, in a small way, wearing a priestly garment. (Emphasis added.)[14]

Some Bible scholars believe that the word translated "hem" in the account of the woman with an issue of blood who touched the Savior's clothing (Matthew 9:20), refers to the Hebrew word *tzitzit* or the fringe discussed in Numbers 15.

In a brochure printed in Jerusalem by *Amutat P'til Tekhelet*, it states: "In ancient times the purple and blue dyes derived from snails were so rare and sought after that they were literally worth their weight in gold. These precious dyes colored the robes of the kings and princes of Media, Babylon, Egypt and Greece. To wear them was to be identified with royalty. Indeed, we are children of the Heavenly King—the tekhelet should remind all of God's children to remember this heritage."

It has been estimated by biblical writers John J. Rousseau and Rami Arav that "the liquid extracted from 12,000 mollusks produced only 1.5 grams of pure purple dye; this explains why a pound of Tyrian purple cost the equivalent of 10,000 dollars (1994 value)."[15]

The *Amutat P'til Tekhelet* brochure continues: "We are commanded to affix a thread of blue to our tsitsit as a constant and conspicuous reminder of our stature. We are *banim lamakom*, the noble sons of the King of the Universe, ever pursuing his mitzvot."

The symbolism of blue is explained by Second Century Rabbi Meir: "The thread of blue in the tzitzit resembles the hue of the sea, the sea mirrors the azure of the sky, and the sky reflects the radiance from the throne of God's glory, concerning which it is written: 'Under His feet . . . a sapphire stone.' "[16]

The late chief Rabbi of Israel, Isaac Herzog, wrote a doctoral thesis in 1913 for the University of London on *The Royal Purple and Biblical Blue: Argaman and Tekhelet*. His thesis was reprinted in 1987 with scientific updates. Rabbi Herzog quotes from Maimonides' Commentary on the Mishnah (completed in 1168 A.D.) on how *tekhelet* is dyed:

"The wool is soaked in chalk and washed until it is clean, and then boiled with *ahla* and the like, as is the practice of the dyers, in order to prepare the wool for absorbing the colour. The blood of the *hilazon* is then put into the vat (kettle) together with drugs such as *kimonia* [cimolia: a cleaning substance to which Pliny refers] as is usual in dyeing; the liquid having been raised to a boiling heat, wool is immersed therein, remaining in that condition until it has the color of the sky, and this is the tekhelet used for the fringes."[17]

Scholars had certain clues from ancient writings about the marine animal called the *Hilazon* which made them think it was the *Murex trunculus*. The *Hilazon* was thought to be a snail (although a certain squid was proposed by the Radzyner Rebbe in the 1800s). The *Murex trunculus* could be found along the northern coast of Israel. It had a shell, though it did not fit the description of the *Hilazon's* body that it was similar to the sea. The dye from the *Hilazon* would create a steadfast color like the sky and sea that was indistinguishable from a vegetable dye called *kala ilan* (indigo). The historian Pliny gave more clues about the dyeing process: "The vein [the hypobranchial gland of the snail which produced the color] is removed . . . and to this salt has to be added . . . three days is the proper time for it to be steeped, and it should be heated in a leaden pot with 50 pounds of dye to every six gallons of water." (Pliny, Natural History 9.61.133)

Since the Murex trunculus snail has an off-white shell with brown stripes which doesn't seem to fit the Talmud's description of similarity to the sea, and because the dye from this snail seems purplish-blue, some experts doubted that this was, indeed, the Hilazon. The booklet published by *Amutat P'Til Tekhelet* explains how it was finally possible to positively identify the Hilazon and to restore the biblical color blue to ritual fringes:

> The shell appears off-white with brown stripes when it is out of the water, cleaned and polished. In its natural element, the *Trunculus* is covered with a coat of sea fouling the color of the ocean. Everything in its vicinity is covered with the same fouling, making it almost impossible to distinguish the snail from the sea bed on which it is found. The Talmud's description is of the *Hilazon* in its natural habitat!
>
> The riddle of producing a pure blue color from the snail was solved serendipitously. While researching the

methods used by the ancient dyers, Prof. Otto Elsner, of the Shekar College of Fibers, noticed that on cloudy days, *Trunculus* dyed tended towards purple, but on sunny days it was a brilliant blue! To the dye masters of old, working in the bright Mediterranean sunlight, this was certainly no secret!" (I obtained this booklet in Jerusalem. If you would like further information you can contact the *Amutat P'Til Tekhelet* organization in the States at 212- 689-7412.)

Jewish historian Nathan Ausubel writes this about the *tzitzit*:

"In the prayer called *Ahabah Rabah* (With Abounding Love), which precedes the recitation of the Shema, the worshiper is required by tradition to gather up all the four tzitzit on his tallit and to petition God: 'O bring us in peace [to Zion] from the four corners of the earth!' Thus the four fringes become poetic symbols of the four corners of the earth—the entire desolate range of the Jewish Dispersion— and not only of God's universal omnipotence."[18]

Aryah Kaplan in his book, *Meditation and Kabbalah,* writes that when the Torah says, "You shall gaze at it [the ritual tassel on the prayer shawl], and remember all of God's commandments," the Talmud is "alluding to the fact that this thread is to be used as an object of meditative contemplation, outlining the steps of spiritual ascent. This thread was colored with a blue dye taken from the *chilazon* . . . the word *chilazon* has the same letters as *la-chazon*, meaning, 'for a vision.' Through this dye, one could attain a vision approaching that of prophecy."[19]

How incredible it is that now Jews from around the world may hold the sky-blue fringe in their *tzitzit* to remember God's commandments and promises to gather them to Jerusalem and to His Holy Temple, may it speedily be rebuilt in our days!

Heifers Pure Red and First-born

And let us not forget that after 2,000 years, it is in <u>our</u> time, in 1994 on a small cattle ranch in Mississippi, in 1997 near Haifa, and in Jerusalem in 2002, that true Red Heifers were announced. And at least two more were born in Texas and in Israel that were not publicized. At this writing, there are three herds of cattle that have produced animals suitable for the Red Heifer sacrifice. This is amazing to me for when I attended the first Temple Conference in Jerusalem in 1992, the talk was still of *possibilities*—from mysterious Swedish herds.

Truly to have pure red calves born is a sign from God that His Temple will now be rebuilt. You will yet see or hear of the sacrifice that will purify the sons of Aaron in preparation for their offerings again unto the Lord.

Now all that remains is a way to begin construction. Will the failed Oslo Accords, the renewed and violent *Intifada* and a hard-line Israeli government be the catalyst for the events that will make construction possible?

The Altar at the Dead Sea

I believe I have saved the most exciting fig leaf for last! I found out about this altar when I was in Jerusalem at The Temple Institute in April, 1998. The Institute's educational director, Raphaella Tabuk, wrote about visiting a "practice" altar in the spring issue of the institute's newsletter, *On the Altar*.

I recently had the opportunity to visit a special site that few have imagined exists. On the sandy grounds of The Dead Sea Works, on the shore of the Dead Sea, stands a full-size model, ten cubits high, of the Temple's Outer Altar. This metal model, as large as a two-story building, was built out of scrap metal on the free time of the workers at the plant. The group I led wanted to learn the steps of the daily service in the Temple by walking through it, and that's what they did. While our eyes followed the points on the handouts, our feet traced the footsteps of the priest walking from the spot where the daily offering would be slaughtered, up the tremendous ramp, and around the designated spots on the top of the altar where the priest would walk.

We felt privileged to trace the steps of so highly-desired a job. When the Temple stood, the priests used to race up the ramp to win the task of offering the tamid, the daily communal offering on the altar. Looking down from high atop the altar, we could understand how it would take good balance to be a priest. . . .

Once we had climbed the ramp, I stepped onto one of the corners of the altar. This is the spot where a priest waved a flag at the moment wine was poured on the altar every morning and evening. When the Levitical orchestra, which stood on a platform near the altar, saw the flag waving, they began to play and sing the song [psalm] of the day.

In the absence of offerings today, we have prayer as a substitute. Before our group left the altar, we prayed the afternoon service on it, facing Jerusalem. The words of the prayer "return the service to Your House . . . and may our eyes behold Your return to Zion" took on a new meaning to us.[20]

With a practice altar in place[21], actual sacrifices were soon to follow. Passover of 1998 is the first time that I am aware of that lambs were sacrificed in Israel. Gershon Salomon was on a tour of the U.S. in June, 1998 and I heard him describe such a sacrifice in Jerusalem. The religious *Yishuv* (community) where I stayed in April 1998, *Mitzpeh Yericho* in the West Bank, also sacrificed a lamb for Pesach.

What a privilege it is to live at this time of incredible restoration! Not only has the Red Heifer been discovered, but all these other Temple preparations as well. Can the Messiah Jews and Christians have been faithfully waiting for be far behind?

1. Quoted in James Kirsch's, *The Reluctant Prophet*, Sherbourne Press, 1973, page 63.
2. Don Stewart and Chuck Missler, *The Coming Temple*, Dart Press, 1991, pages 194-196.
3. Chuck Missler, *The Second Annual Jerusalem Temple Conference*, 8 cassette tapes with notes, Koinonia House, 1993, pages 11-16.
4. From Sagiv's booklet, *The Hidden Secrets of the Temple Mount*, printed in Jerusalem.
5. James Fleming, "The Undisclosed Gate Beneath Jerusalem's Golden Gate," *Biblical Archaeology Review*, January/February, 1983, page 30.
6. Hal Lindsey, *A Prophetical Walk Through the Holy Land*, Harvest House Publishers, Second Edition, 1987, page 75.
7. Rabbi Israel Ariel, translated and adapted by Rabbi Chaim Richman, *The Odyssey of the Third Temple*, Israel Publications & Productions, Jerusalem, Av 5753 (1992) page 102.
8. Alfred Edersheim, *The Temple: Its Ministry and Service*, Wm. B. Eerdmans Publishing Company, 1987, page 215.
9. Eliyahu Kitov, *The Book of Our Heritage*, Vol. II, Adar-Nisan, Feldheim Publishers, Jerusalem/New York, 1978, pages 226-227.
10. Ibid, page 236.
11. Joachim Jeremias, *Jerusalem in the Time of Jesus*, Fortress Press, Philadelphia, 1969, page 214.
12. Grant R. Jeffrey, "A Genetic Trace is Found Linking Kohanim Worldwide," No. Y66, *The Y Files*, (www.Yfiles.com).
13. *Midrash Rabbah*, Numbers, Vol. 2, translated by Judah J. Slotki, M.A., Soncino Press, 1983, page 705.
14. Jacob Milgrom, "Of Hems and Tassels: Rank, Authority and Holiness Were Expressed in Antiquity by Fringes on Garments," *Biblical Archaeology Review*, May/June 1983, page 65.
15. John J. Rousseau and Rami Arav, *Jesus and His World: An Archaeological and Cultural Dictionary*, Fortress Press, Minneapolis, 1995, page 315.
16. Second-century Rabbi Meir as quoted in Nathan Ausebel, *The Book of Jewish Knowledge*, Crown Publishers, Inc., New York, 1973, page 485.
17. Maimonides as quoted in *The Royal Purple and the Biblical Blue" The Study of Chief Rabbi Isaac Herzog and Recent Scientific Contributions*, Editor Ehud Spanier, Keter Publishing House Jerusalem Ltd., 1987, page 142.
18. Nathan Ausubel, *The Book of Jewish Knowledge*, page 486.
19. Aryah Kaplan, *Meditatian and Kabbalah*, Samuel Weiser, York Beach, Maine, 1982, page 79.
20. Raphaella Tabak, Education Director of the Temple Institute, in *On the Altar*, printed in Jerusalem, Spring 1998, Vol. I, Issue 2, page 6.
21. I heard that during the administration of Israeli Prime Minister Ehud Barak, this altar was dismantled. But after Barak's defeat at the polls in February 2001, the Likud's new Prime Minister Ariel Sharon may allow religious observances to move forward once again. And at a lecture on February 25, 2001, archaeologist Vendyl Jones reported that the practice altar was not dismantled and is in use for teaching the sacrificial system.

Chapter Four

David and Jonathan: Rabbi Chaim Richman and Clyde Lott

Behold, how good and how pleasant it is for brethren to dwell together in unity!—Psalms 133:1.

A more unlikely friendship could not be imagined: an Orthodox Jew from Jerusalem and a Pentecostal cattle rancher from Canton, Mississippi. But Clyde Lott and Chaim Richman became like brothers. That these two men of God would come together because of a Red Heifer is even more incredible. Putting aside religious differences, these two men worked side-by-side to assist God in bringing about the redemption of the world through the building of the Third Temple in Jerusalem. Both men await the coming of the Messiah and a future era of world peace.

We often think callings from God are dramatic and grandiose: like Constantine seeing a blazing cross in the sky and hearing the words: "By this go forth and conquer." But more often one receives quiet promptings from the "still, small voice." And that's exactly how the Rev. Clyde Lott was moved to become a "Righteous Gentile" for Jews seeking to re-establish Temple worship.

The Gentleman Rancher

Rabbi Chaim Richman paid a supreme compliment to the Mississippi cattle rancher named Clyde Lott. He said, "This is a person without guile." The term "Southern Gentleman" is applicable as well to describe this soft-spoken, kindly man. Rev. Lott was raised on a purebred cattle farm and majored in animal science at Hinds Junior College and Mississippi State University. While at MSU the livestock judging team he was on won first place in the nation. Rev. Lott later directed the marketing

Reverend Clyde Lott

of livestock to 4-H and Future Farmers of America in the Southeastern United States and bred and marketed many different types of cattle on the local, state and national level. Many of his cattle were judged champions.

Rev. Lott is married to Priscilla Taylor and they have a two children. An ordained minister with the Pentecostal Assemblies of Jesus Christ, Rev. Lott raises Red Angus cattle on his ranch in Canton, Mississippi.

It Started with the Bible

The Red Heifer project began one day in Lott's study more than ten years ago with Jacob's spotted and speckled cattle. "I was studying Genesis 30:32 about the different colored cattle that Jacob received from Laban and the question came to my mind that if these were the foundational cattle of Israel, how would they produce a Red Heifer? You can't consistently produce red except from red to black or black to red with a black recessive gene," Lott told me. Lott knows cattle, especially his Red Angus cattle with their deep reddish coloring. Indeed, how could Israel produce this needed heifer? Lott found the question weighing heavily on his heart.

One day in 1990 he felt compelled to drive to Jackson to the office of Roy D. Manning, Director of International Trade for the Mississippi Department of Agriculture. In a New Yorker interview, Lott said, "I will never forget as long as I live walking into Mr. Manning's office that day . . . and saying, 'I have read the Bible and the Bible says Israel has to have a Red Heifer.' "[1] Manning drafted a letter that went to the agricultural attache' at the American Embassy in Athens, Greece, then to the State Department, next to the American Embassy in Tel Aviv, where it was finally routed to The Temple Institute in Jerusalem and into the capable hands of Rabbi Chaim Richman.

Manning's letter said he had been approached by a producer and seller of cattle from the State of Mississippi who said he could provide: "Red Angus cattle suitable for Old Testament Biblical sacrifices," and these cattle would have no blemishes or off-color hair. "These cattle will adapt quickly to Middle Eastern climate, also excellent beef quality."

In Rabbi Richman's book, *The Mystery of the Red Heifer: Divine Promise of Purity*, he calls this episode "A Letter Goes Lost: Around the World in 90 Days." But no matter how long it took, this letter was vital to the restoration of Temple worship in Israel—all because one quietly humble cattleman in Mississippi listened to the quiet promptings of the Holy Spirit. But not only was there a Christian in Canton, Mississippi listening to the Holy Spirit, there was a Jewish scholar in Jerusalem also tuned into this Source.

Chaim Richman: For Such a Time As This

Mordecai's words to Esther, "and who knoweth whether thou are come to the kingdom for such a time as this?" were tailor-made for the scholarly Rabbi Chaim Richman. Born in Massachusetts, Rabbi Richman and his family moved to Israel in 1982. He served The Temple Institute as both the director and head of research. Rabbi Richman translated and adapted the epic work *The Odyssey of the Third Temple* written by the founder of The Temple Institute, Rabbi Yisrael Ariel. Rabbi Ariel was among the paratroopers who wept and prayed at the Western Wall on that June day in 1967 when Israel regained access to her holy sites in East Jerusalem.

Rabbi Richman also wrote *The Holy Temple of Jerusalem* and *The Temple Haggadah,* making him an internationally acclaimed authority on the Temple.

In 1992, Rabbi Richman addressed a gathering of Evangelical Christians at a Temple Conference held at the Jerusalem Hilton. Later, the group toured The Temple Institute under the rabbi's direction. I was mightily blessed to attend this conference and found the rabbi's knowledge of the Sacrifice of the Red Heifer simply encyclopedic.

For many of the group at the Temple Conference, this was their first exposure to Orthodox Judaism. When one man asked the rabbi, "What will your Messiah be like?" Rabbi Richman bristled just a bit as he replied, "Don't say *your* Messiah; he will be a global Messiah and will spiritually rectify all mankind." Meeting this group of enthusiastic Christians seemed almost like an occupational hazard for the rabbi.

Perhaps those early encounters with devout Christians prepared Rabbi Richman for his encounter with the cattle rancher from Mississippi who held a key to the Red Heifer.

Once Rabbi Richman had received the fateful letter, there were phone calls from Jerusalem to Canton, Mississippi which led to Rev. Lott flying to Israel to meet Rabbi Richman. It's one thing to understand someone else's religion from what you have heard or read about them. It's quite another thing to be immersed in their culture. Walking through The Temple Institute with Rabbi Richman was a life-changing experience Rev. Lott said. In turn, the rabbis learned about Pentecostal belief in Jesus, being anointed by the Spirit and speaking in tongues.

Rev. Lott and the Righteous Gentile from Ashkelon

At the Temple Institute, much attention was paid to the Rev. Clyde Lott's last name. And it was not because of Trent Lott, the U.S. Senate Majority Leader! The Rabbis were thinking of the biblical Lot (Abraham's nephew) who was a Gentile and an excellent cattle breeder. It seemed more than a coincidence for a Gentile named Lott to be speaking of bringing Israel a Red Heifer.

For there is a rabbinic tradition that a Gentile named Dama ben Netinah did that very thing. The story is told that a stone had fallen out of the breastplate of the High Priest and the gentile jeweler Dama ben Netinah of Ashkelon had a precious stone for sale as a replacement.

The rabbis traveled to Ashkelon and agreed to a price for the stone. When Dama went to get it for them, he found that his father had fallen asleep with his leg on the chest where the gem was stored. He would not disturb his father's sleep. Though the price had been set at a thousand gold pieces, the rabbis thought Dama was stalling to get them to pay a higher price, so they offered ten thousand gold pieces. When his father awoke, Dama brought out the gemstone, but when the rabbis offered him the higher price, he said, "Heaven forfend! I will not make a profit out of honoring my parents; I will only take from you the first price, one thousand gold pieces, which I had fixed with you." The story says that the reward given Dama by the Holy One, blessed be He, is that "in the very same year his cow did give birth to a red heifer which he sold for more than ten thousand gold pieces."[2]

Lawrence Wright reported in the New Yorker that during Rev. Lott's meeting with the rabbis gathered at The Temple Institute, he was asked how much one of his purebred Red Angus would cost. Rev. Lott said two thousand dollars a head. As Rabbi Richman translated the amount into Hebrew, it caused a commotion among the rabbis. When Rev. Lott asked what was the matter, Rabbi Richman said that twenty thousand a head was a lot of money. Rev. Lott exclaimed that he hadn't said twenty thousand, he said two thousand and that he wouldn't take advantage of them as they were seeking to turn back to God.

The rabbis were amazed. That conversation had incredible echoes of the ancient sages with Dama ben Netinah. While the rabbis were astonished, Rev. Lott was deeply touched to think that 2,500 years later, the Righteous Gentile scene was being played out again. But this time, the Righteous Gentile would provide not only a Red Heifer, but a whole herd of vigorous beef cattle for the land of Israel.

The connection between Rev. Lott and Dama ben Netinah wasn't the only incident with such resonance. As I visited with Rev. Lott he told me that while sitting in Rabbi Ariel's office, he was asked to look over a map of Israel and suggest places where his Red Angus herd could be placed to the best advantage. Rev. Lott chose four places, and looking up, noticed that Rabbi Ariel was very quiet. Three times the rabbi said to Rev. Lott: "Do you know what you have done?" Rev. Lott replied, "We've just chosen some land for the cows." Rabbi Ariel then said, "You have chosen the same path Abraham, Isaac and Jacob followed when they came into the Land." Rev. Lott felt like that from that standpoint, his Red Angus cattle "could be leading the Bible back to the world."

Now it was Rabbi Richman's turn to travel to the Bible Belt to meet with Rev. Lott and see his Red Angus cattle. The rabbi journeyed to the lush countryside of Mississippi to inspect the first-born, never-yoked, pure-red heifer raised by Rev. Lott. And on November 11, 1994, Rabbi Richman said, "This is the heifer that will change the world."

But the connection between Rev. Lott and Rabbi Richman has come to mean more for Israel than just providing a Red Heifer. Rabbi Richman has written: ". . . what began as a quest to provide a red heifer fitting for the Third Temple has blossomed into a much larger vision: a plan dedicated to aiding the total economic advancement of the people and State of Israel through the importation of these cattle. . .With success, the operation will actually transform Israel from a country dependent on importing inferior beef from other countries, to a leading exporter in her own right."[3]

In a telephone interview from Rev. Lott's home in 1997, Rabbi Richman explained to me why this Red Heifer project could have dual goals: "Even in the time of the Second Temple, the Temple functioned as a social watch. It was instrumental in just plain helping out the people economically." The rabbi said that Rev. Lott's beef cattle herd "is no less Messianic and no less redemptive than the Red Heifer on the road to Messiah."

An organization called "Canaan Land Restoration of Israel, Inc." was formed to facilitate moving Rev. Lott's Red Angus herds to Israel. Rev.

Lott was president; Guy Garner Jr., vice president; Rabbi Richman served as director and Alfred Bishop as secretary/treasurer.

The non-profit organization is concerned with every aspect of settling Red Angus cattle in Israel. Rev. Lott's concern for the Israel-bound cattle extends even to the proper forage grasses to feed the cattle. In a letter to Rabbi Ariel of the Temple Institute, Rev. Lott wrote: "We must get the herds of red cattle from the United States to Israel, and we must also feed them. Therefore, we will use forage (grasses) developed in the United States for barren land. These deep-rooted grasses will look for water table to a depth of over 25 feet. They will, therefore, draw water to the surface, causing pools and streams to collect where only before barren land was seen. This will surely fulfill the word of G-d as recorded in Isaiah 35."

Rabbi Richman and Rev. Lott had many meetings with agriculture officials in the U.S. and in Israel and with kibbutz leaders of possible ranch locations.

Rev. Lott now serves as a board member on the National Agricultural Steering Committee (of Israel), the association founded by AMBAL (the Association of Beef Cattle Breeders in Israel) for the purpose of restoring red cattle to the land of Abraham, Isaac and Jacob.

If you feel led to assist Rev. Lott in this project, you may contact Rev. Lott at: 270 Moss Road, Canton, MS 39046.

Rev. Lott shared with me the following letter dated January 7, 1999 from Rabbi Yisrael Ariel, founder of The Temple Institute:

> Greetings from Jerusalem!
>
> I was pleased to meet with you in The Temple Institute on Monday, January 4, 1999. I am proud of the relationship The Temple Institute has developed with Canaan Land Restoration of Israel Inc., over the past eight years. Our partnership has two chief aims: restoring the red heifer to Israel after 2,000 years since the destruction of the Holy Temple and revitalizing cattle raising throughout Israel.

We are glad to see that after years of effort on your part, this dream is becoming a reality. Large herds of red cow[s] will soon be on their way to the ancient grazing lands of the Golan, the Gilboa [southern Galilee] and the hills of Jerusalem

We commend you on your work and wish you success in all of your endeavors. We pray that through the commandment of the red heifer, whose ashes were traditionally prepared on the Mount of Olives, facing the Temple Mount, purity will soon return to Israel.

Respectfully,
Yisrael Ariel
Founder of The Temple Institute
Jerusalem[4]

A Light to the Nations

Rabbi Richman's work with Clyde Lott has fulfilled some very particular promptings from the *Ruach HaKodesh*, the Holy Spirit of God. He writes in his book, "It had been in my mind for some time to find a way of building a bridge of understanding between Jews and Christians. . . The many years of experiences and relationships I forged at the Temple Institute taught me that the time had come for emphasizing the common Biblical goals which we all must share for the future redemption and the unfolding of God's plan for mankind."[5]

Rabbi Richman's website is "A Light to the Nations" (www.lttn.org) and it underscores his belief that the coming Temple is more than a magnificent synagogue or building. "It's the place where G-d can rest His presence on Mount Moriah," the rabbi told me. "The Temple: I view it as the hope of Mankind," he said. "And the Red Heifer is the single-most important development in the saga of the Temple. It's the missing ingredient to purity today."

Rabbi Richman has been in the perfect position to begin building that bridge. He has fulfilled speaking engagements across the United States throughout the 1990s, sharing how God is moving among the nations with Pentecostals, Methodists, Baptists, Evangelicals and many other faiths. I have been able to attend several of these meetings and have found an incredible spirit of God emanating from the rabbi as he explains how Israel is turning back to God.

A friend at Hebrew University in Jerusalem e-mailed me news that Rabbi Richman would be speaking in the U.S. during the month of May, 1997. I made some phone calls and arranged to be in Thomastown, Mississippi to hear the rabbi and to meet the Rev. Clyde Lott.

The Pentecostal Wake Forest Church was jammed two hours before the rabbi arrived. This was my first experience with Pentecostal worship and I kept wondering how Rabbi Richman would react to the rapturous worship services. I needn't have worried. As the Pentecostals reached out to welcome "Brother Chaim," he responded with warmth and graciousness.

A bridge of understanding was built between Christian and Jew that night. The congregation listened intently as Rabbi Richman explained the significance of the Red Heifer and the coming of the Messiah. The rabbi noted that up until now, dialogue between Christian and Jew had only been about the things that separate us. It was now time to look at the things we have in common: a love of God and living a life of righteousness.

Again the question of "your" Messiah came up. Rabbi Richman said, "That really offends me. He's the Messiah for the whole earth!" Then he said that our religious differences would become a moot issue when Messiah comes. "Jews will be Jews and Christians will be Christians. Then let's let God be God," the rabbi said.

I, for one, could hardly believe my ears when Rabbi Richman quoted from the New Testament. In Acts 15:13-19, Paul and Barnabas are meeting with James and the Jerusalem church where it is spoken: "Wherefore my sentence is that we trouble not them, which from among the Gentiles are turned to God." Rabbi Richman said these were the gentile God-fearers of Jesus' time. He said that as Jew and Gentile, we need to be really united at this time. "There is a decision or challenge that faces everyone: Will we be or not be on the side of God?" Rabbi Richman asked the congregation.

Rev. Lott shared with me his new insights into Jewish-Christian relationships. "Up until this point, the Christians have wanted to rah-rah Jesus' name to the Jew and tell him that he's going to hell. But God is a greater God than that. We try to downsize God to our own carnal state when the Word does tell us that God's ways are not our ways. We've got to get beyond our own religious views and work together. God has got a plan for man and God's plan is in action. If we obey the basic commandments and love one another, we can give God the opportunity to be God and reveal his own plans for mankind."

Rev. Lott made one more comment that Christians would do well to ponder. "In the Millennium, with the festivals, feasts and sabbaths, the 'Gentile' world will look much more Jewish." Some Christians may scoff at this, but it is absolutely true. One of the few scriptures that discusses the Millennial reign of Christ, tells us that those who survive the Second Coming will be under commandment to observe the Feast of Tabernacles as in days of old. Consider Zechariah 14:16-19:

> And it shall come to pass, that every one that is left of all the nations which came up against Jerusalem shall even go up from year to year to worship the King, the Lord of hosts, and to keep the feast of tabernacles. And it shall be, that whoso will not come up of all the families of the earth unto Jerusalem to worship the King, the Lord of hosts, even upon them shall be no rain. And if the family of Egypt go not up, and come not, that have no rain; there shall be the plague, wherewith the Lord will smite the heathen that come not up to keep the feast of tabernacles. This shall be the punishment of Egypt, and the punishment of all nations that come not up to keep the feast of tabernacles.

Rev. Lott is a man who lives by the Word of God. Of his friendship with a rabbi from Jerusalem, Rev. Lott said, "My background in no way prepared me for meeting Rabbi Richman, but I felt God in it. God has been the orchestrator of our friendship and has taken that relationship and broadened and deepened it. It's all been God and in some ways, it's like a Jonathan and David relationship."

More on the Red Heifer/Land of Canaan Project

I spoke with Rev. Lott at the end of October, 1999 to ask him about the planned shipment of his Red Angus cattle. He said there was a 50-50 chance that they would be shipped by the end of that December. (It did not happen.) "We're not 100 percent sure—it's God's timing. But we're directly involved with the settlements [in Israel where the cattle will be pastured] and with the government." Rev. Lott said that the project was now a complicated cattle affair and that Rabbi Richman was back doing the research he loves at the Temple Institute. While Rev. Lott was in Omaha, Nebraska filming a special for PBS, the Lord was "leading people to get involved in helping get the cattle to Israel," said Rev. Lott. "We walk by faith and let the Holy Spirit guide us."

Preparing for the Sacrifice

One question that Rabbi Richman is asked constantly, is how will the officiating priest for the Red Heifer sacrifice be cleansed from the death impurity that has come upon Jews since the destruction of the Temple? This priest must be ritually pure or he will invalidate the sacrifice. Will the Jews need to recover ashes from Second Temple times?

Rabbi Richman is skeptical of Vendyl Jones's search for the ancient ashes (discussed in the following chapter). He said to me he was concerned about the purity of ancient ashes should they be found. How would one know whether or not the ashes had been rendered unclean by Gentile handling? Jones has suggested that the *kalal* (the Hebrew name of the vessel named in the Mishnah as containing the ashes) will be sealed with the imprint of the High Priest. Rabbi Richman found that rather ludicrous. He drew a comparison between Jones' suggestion and a Catholic Cardinal sealing something in wax with the imprint of his ring! Not very likely.

However, I found just such a reference in Judaism. The word *Gemara* is Aramaic for "completion." The Gemara is commentary on the Mishnah; the Gemara and the Mishnah make up the Talmud. In the Gemara there is an account of the origin of Hanukkah, the Feast of Lights that celebrates the overthrow of Syrian King Antiochus Epiphanes:

> For when the idolators entered the Temple, they defiled all the oils in the Temple. When the Hasmonean dynasty gained the upper hand and conquered them, they searched and found only one cruse of oil sealed with the seal of the High Priest. It contained only sufficient oil for one day, but a miracle happened to it, and they lit eight days from it. The next year, they fixed these days as festive days of praise and thanksgiving.[5]

Rabbi Richman believes there is a solution for this purity problem that is not tied in with the discovery of ancient ashes. He stated that the pure waters of Shiloach could be sprinkled upon the officiating priest. The waters could be guaranteed pure if collected in a manner outlined in the Mishnah and described by Maimonides.

Moses Maimonides, who lived from 1136-1204 C.E., was one of the greatest writers on the Law. Maimonides wrote about the Mishnah's description of children born and raised in purity in Jerusalem in Temple times. These children would provide the way to purify the officiating priest without ancient Red Heifer ashes:

> And how could anyone be found who had never suffered corpse uncleanliness? There were courtyards in Jerusalem

built over rock and beneath them the rock was hollowed out for fear of any grave down in the depths; and they used to bring children and there they reared them. When it was desired to sprinkle the priest who should burn the red heifer oxen were brought—because their bellies are distended—and boards were put on their backs and the children sat on the boards so that there should be a "tent" intervening between them and the ground, for fear of any grave down in the depths; they held stone jugs in their hands, and thus they made their way to Siloam. When they reached Siloam they alighted and drew water—for there was no need for scruple lest there should be any grave there in the depths, since it is not men's habit to bury beneath rivers. Then they got up again and sat on the boards and went on until they reached the Temple Mount. When they reached the Temple Mount they alighted and walked on their own feet, since below the whole of the Temple Mount and the Temple Courts was a hollowed space for fear of any grave down in the depths. They went along to the gate of the Temple Court; and at the gate of the court was a jar of ashes. <u>They took the ashes and put them in the water that was in the stone jugs and sprinkled it upon the priest who should burn the red heifer.</u>[6] (Emphasis added.)

The International Jerusalem Post featured an article about this procedure (week ending March 14, 1998.) It stated that many religious Jews were asking the question, "What happens if we have a red heifer—but don't have anybody in the state of purity to handle its ashes?" Jerusalem Post writer Herb Keinon noted: "The idea arose of establishing a compound where babies whose fathers are kohanim [priests] would be born and raised until bar-mitzvah age. . . The children will remain in the compound until a red heifer is found, after which they will prepare the mixture that will purify the Jewish people and enable them to go onto the Temple and Mount and enter areas that to date have been halachically off limits." Keinon reported that Rabbi Yosef Elboim, of Jerusalem's *Yeshivat Torat Habayit* (which deals exclusively with laws pertaining to the Temple) said in March of 1998, "There is a woman interested and the project is due to start in about two months."

Rabbi Richman believes that such young men could sprinkle the spring waters of Shiloach on an officiating priest which would enable him to offer the Red Heifer in purity.

Another witness for the rabbi's views is found in *The Book of Our Heritage* where it explains how the *Cohen Gadol* (the High Priest) who would sacrifice the Red Heifer was sequestered for seven days in a special stone chamber in the Temple. (The stone prevented defilement.)

> Each of the seven days some of the remaining ashes of all the previous 'heifers' was sprinkled on the designated cohen, in order to purify him from any unknown defilement.
>
> Only such a person who had never been defiled by contact with the dead could sprinkle ashes on the designated cohen. Likewise, the vessels used for the sprinkling were required to be of stone (which could never be defiled). [Emphasis added.][7]

"For With God Nothing Shall Be Impossible." Luke 1:37

In the early years of my research on the Red Heifer, I read a story in the International Jerusalem Post (week ending August 19, 1989) about possible red heifers coming from South Africa or from Sweden. Rabbi Menahem Burstein is one of the foremost experts on Temple worship. Joel Rebibo reported that Rabbi Burstein "is convinced that genetic engineering can produce a kosher red heifer required for Temple services. His worldwide search is part of his attempt to demystify the ritual of animal sacrifice." (Emphasis added.)

Isn't it incredible that faithful Jews did not have to depend on man's technology? Could any man do what God has done in engineering a gene in the DNA of all Cohens so that their priestly heritage "reverberates on a biological level" as Rabbi Richman described it? And now it is in God's perfect timing to send Red Heifers to Israel. Not just one but several. We are truly in the time of redemption. Blessed be the Name of God!

A Disheartening Postscript

It would have been lovely to end this chapter with the previous paragraph. But the reality of life is that the adversary tries to disrupt the work of men who are trying to do God's will.

Rabbi Richman and Rev. Lott had differences of opinion regarding the Red Heifer project and are no longer working together. Both continue to speak kindly to me of the other in conversations I have had with them. But Rabbi Richman is now working with Israeli cattlemen regarding a Red Heifer with apparent success as announced in April 2002.

But it seems that feelings have run much deeper than I was told. Gershom Gorenberg, *Jerusalem Report* senior editor and columnist, wrote that although Rabbi Richman had once said of Rev. Lott, " 'I feel closer to him than I do to some of my own family'. . . at the end of 1998, the Jerusalem rabbi angrily broke his connection with Canaan Land Restoration. The immediate dispute was financial. A later letter from Richman suggests an additional cause for tension—an allegation that Lott had been filmed in a Florida church talking about spreading the Gospel in Israel."[8]

And Rev. Lott's organization has also undergone a legal trial. There was a lawsuit against the former vice president of the organization, the Rev. Guy Garner, over questions as to who should lead the project and who would control it.

In an article in *The Messianic Times*, it was reported that "A Mississippi judge issued a permanent restraining order against Garner, who was removed from his position, and ordered him to return the organization's

[Land of Canaan's] computer and bank records."[9] In a March 4, 2001 phone conversation from his ranch in Mississippi, Rev. Lott said that the legal issues were settled in his favor and he is moving ahead with his plans to give Israel a herd of his prize-winning Red Angus cattle. "If a person's motives are not what the Lord deems right, that person will be taken out of the picture," Rev. Lott told me.

A new organization, "Lott's Cattle, Inc." has been formed and will continue the dream of the Gentile cattle rancher named Lott. In spite of the fact of the recent Israeli Red Heifer, will Rabbi Richman see another kosher Red Heifer from those Mississippi Red Angus cattle? Rev. Lott told me that regardless of the Red Heifer announced by Rabbi Richman in April 2002, he still feels the call to provide cattle for Israel. It seems this is one "fig leaf" we will have to wait and watch for.

---

1. Lawrence Wright, "Forcing the End," *The New Yorker*, July 20, 1998, page 44.

2. *Midrash Rabbah*, The Soncino Press, London, New York, 1983, Vol. 7, page 16.

3. Rabbi Chaim Richman, *The Mystery of the Red Heifer: Divine Promise of Purity*, Jerusalem, 1997, page 71.

4. Letter from Rev. Clyde Lott to Rabbi Yisrael Ariel of the Temple Institute, dated March 10, 1999, facsimile copy in the author's possession.

5. Gemara from *Megillah Ta'anith*, Shabbath, 21b, quoted in *Sabbath Shiurim*, by Rabbi M. Miller, G.J. George and Co., Ltd., London, 1979, page 61.

6. Moses Maimonides, *The Code of Maimonides*, Book X, "The Book of Cleanness," translated from the Hebrew by Herbert Danby, Yale University Press, New Haven, 1954, page 102.

7. Eliyahu Kitov, *The Book of Our Heritage*, Feldheim Publishers, Jerusalem, New York, 1978, Vol. II, *Adar-Nisan*, pages 107-108.

8. Gershom Gorenberg, *The End of Days: Fundamentalism and the Struggle for the Temple Mount*, The Free Press, a Division of Simon & Schuster Inc., New York, 2000.

9. Karen Boren, "Dispute Delays Red Heifer Delivery," *The Messianic Times*, English Edition, Vol. 10, Number 2, Spring 2000, page 3.

Chapter Five

Vendyl Jones and the Kalal

Dilettantes, dilettantes!—is what those who pursue a science or an art for love and the delight they take in it . . . are disdainfully called by those who pursue it only for gain, because they delight only in the money that is to be made . . . Only the man who cares about something in itself, who loves it and does it con amore, will do it in all seriousness. The highest achievement has always been that of such men, and not of the hacks who serve for pay.
— Philosopher Arthur Schopenhauer.

Vendyl Jones has devoted his life's work to a search for Temple artifacts—in particular the Ashes of the Red Heifer—using the Copper Scroll as his guide. To understand the man, you must know something about this ancient document.

The Copper Scroll is the only Dead Sea Scroll that was made of metal. It was found at Cave 3 at Qumran in 1952. In an overview of the Copper Scroll that he was asked to write for the forthcoming *Encyclopedia of the Dead Sea Scrolls* (ed. Lawrence H. Schiffman and James C. VanderKam; New York: Oxford Press, Inc.), scroll scholar Al Wolters wrote that the scroll has a definite structure by which it is organized. "In an unvarying pattern, the 64 sections present material in the following order:

(1) a designation of a hiding place

(2) a further specification of the hiding place

(3) a command to dig or measure

(4) a distance expressed in cubits

(5) a treasure description

(6) additional comments

(7) Greek letters[1]

Wolters called the scroll "the most enigmatic of the Dead Sea Scrolls"—noting that it was a list of hidden treasures punched out in Hebrew on thin copper sheets.

Back in the 1960s when scholars were still calling the Copper Scroll folklore, Jones earned the scorn of the scholarly community for believing the message of the scroll was real, not some wild fiction. The reaction he received was immediate and scornful. "Imagine trying to use an ancient document to find Israel's Temple treasures!" (Never mind that the ancient city of Ubar was found by studying Pliny and then using NASA satellite imagery to pinpoint the site.)

Vendyl Jones interpreting the Copper Scroll for dig volunteers

"It goes almost without saying that the document [Copper Scroll] is not an historical record of actual treasures buried in antiquity. The characteristics of the document itself, not to mention the fabulous quantity of precious metals and treasures recorded in it, place it firmly in the genre of folklore,"[2] said Father J.T. Milik, the scholar assigned to publish the scroll. (Some scholars were not so tactful and called the scroll a "hoax.")

But Vendyl Jones stubbornly pursued his study of the Copper Scroll, believing it to be a document meant to be taken seriously.

The Digger from Texas

Jones is an enigma himself. Try to describe him! You can say he's Texas-born, a former Baptist minister, founder of *B'Nai Noach* (a form of Judaism for Gentiles), Copper Scroll expert, bane of the Israel Antiquities Authority and most important of all (and the part that his detractors like to gloss over), the discoverer of ancient Temple artifacts.

I might add that Jones and I do not entirely share the same theological viewpoint. We both love and honor God. But I believe that Jesus Christ is the Son of God and Jones adheres to Judaism. Through the years of writing about Vendyl Jones, spending time with him and going on one of his digs, a very dear friendship has developed. I have a lot of respect for the tenaciousness Jones has shown in following his "mandate" or calling to pursue the Ashes of the Red Heifer. He has given more than 30 years of his life to this pursuit. I have absolutely no question of this man's integrity and devotion to God.

Jones was born in 1930 and his biography tells of his early love of archaeology, excavating Indian burial sites near his home town of Sudan, Texas.

The biography states that he attended Southwestern Theological Seminary, received a Baccalaureate of Divinity and a Master's Degree of Theology from The Bible Baptist Seminary. He worked at the Bowen Biblical Museum under the direction of curator Dr. William Bowen and his wife. The Bowens were students and associates of the late W.M. Petrie, Egyptologist and biblical archaeologist W.F. Albright.

But following Jones' Southern Baptist schooling, he walked away from the pastorate of Dungan Chapel Baptist Church located on the border of Virginia and North Carolina in 1956. Jones says he was bothered by anti-Jewish statements in the New Testament. He began Talmud Torah studies with Rabbi Henry Barneis in Greenville, South Carolina and also with Rabbi Max Stauber in Spartanburg.

From 1964 to 1967 Jones lectured for the Biblical Research Society and founded the Judaic-Christian Research foundation which in turn birthed Jones's Institute of Judaic-Christian Research. (Now known as Vendyl Jones Research Institutes, Inc.)

In April of 1967, Jones moved his family to Israel. He was the first non-Jew to be accepted at the Department of Judaica at Hebrew University. Harold Mason, head of the American Friends of Hebrew University said to Vendyl: "You were the first non-Jew to study Judaism at Hebrew University, but you were not the last. You have blazed the trail that thousands have followed."[3]

During the Six Day War, Jones was the only American to fight with the Israelis (see *Time* magazine, June 16, 1967). He also studied at the Lubavitcher Yeshiva in Jerusalem and with noted Kabbalist Haim Shivilli. From this background you may now understand that Vendyl Jones is steeped in Judaism, especially Rabbinic Judaism.

Jones considered the late Israeli archaeologist Pesach bar Adon his mentor and the two ranged far and wide in the Judean wilderness. They were excavating and investigating in the wilderness near Qumran before the road there was even built. Jones's excavations in 1977, 1978, 1982 and 1989 were with bar Adon. Jones's biography also notes he worked at Tel Debir with professor Moshe Kohavi and Anson Rainey, the University of Tel Aviv and the Citadel of Herod in Jerusalem with Rabbi Hillel Geva. Vendyl Jones has been able to mount 14 digs in Israel, raising at least $2 million to fund the excavations and for the equipment that makes cave digs possible (including a ventilation system and conveyor belt to assist in removing rubble and rock).

I first learned of Jones in a May 20, 1989 Associated Press article by Mary Sedor in which she wrote:

> For 21 years, Texan Vendyl Jones has been using the Dead Sea Scrolls like a treasure map to search surrounding desert caves for riches of the Jewish Temple buried by the ancient Israelis.
>
> Among the lost artifacts Jones hopes to recover are the "Ashes of the Red Heifer." . . . Jones believes he had been

able to locate the cave where the Temple treasures are buried. "The scroll says that on the way from Jericho to the biblical town of Secacah, in the Wadi of the Dome, there lies . . . a cave with two openings separated by a large column." said Jones . . . "It says this is the cave where the treasures are buried."

Jones and his son, Wain, began excavating the cave in 1977. Within a few months 30 buckets full of pottery and other artifacts were unearthed.

In 1992, Jones did an interview with a Salt Lake City radio station and I called in to get his telephone number. I learned that Vendyl Jones had indeed used the Copper Scroll to find Temple artifacts. On his 1988 dig, his volunteer workers uncovered a tiny clay jar wrapped in palm leaves. Archaeologist Joseph Patrick, whom Jones paid to be the Israeli expert on the dig, announced after extensive tests (which Jones paid for) that the jar contained the oil used to anoint the Hebrew kings and priests.

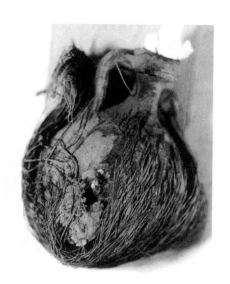

Juglet of holy anointing oil found by Vendyl Jones

When the dig was written up for the Sept./Oct. 1989 *Biblical Archaeology Review*, Patrick "forgot" to mention just who sponsored it. (And the irony is that Patrick wasn't even present when the juglet was uncovered.) No mention was made at all of Vendyl Jones and the volunteers who paid their own way to Israel to search for the Ashes of the Red Heifer. That incident proved to be prophetic regarding how Jones would be treated by 'the establishment.' When Jones attended a seminar on the 40th anniversary of the unrolling of the Copper Scroll in Manchester, England in 1996, although he paid the fee like everyone else, those in charge of the conference refused to give him the CD-ROM with new photographs of the Copper Scroll that other attendees received. "Loose cannon," "Vandal Jones" are some the nicer epithets he has had thrown his way.

As an aside, I also would like to mention that Jones seems to be the only Copper Scroll scholar who has noticed that noted Israeli archaeologist Yigael Yadin wrote in his "Temple Scroll" translation that a list of "altar utensils" in the Temple Scroll was similar to one found in the Copper Scroll. (See Table 6, page 229 of Vol. I of Yadin's *The Temple Scroll,* The Institute of Archaeology of the Hebrew University of Jerusalem, Jerusalem, 1963). This seems yet another confirmation that the Copper Scroll is more than folklore.

Temple Incense Found at Qumran

Vendyl and the incense found at the Cave of the Column

Ignoring the scholarly criticism, Jones kept returning to Israel to dig. In 1992 he and his volunteers uncovered some 800 pounds of incense at the north entrance to the "Cave of the Column" at Qumran.

No one, Dead Sea scholar or otherwise, can deny that the Copper Scroll mentions a site with the following description exactly fitting Jones's Cave of the Column: "In the cave of the pillar—the one having the two openings and facing east—in the northern opening dig three cubits" Column Six, lines 1-4, Copper Scroll (exact wording most translations).

Jones located a cave of two openings with a massive "pillar" between. He also located a north opening to this same cave. And this is where the incense was found, carefully buried under what archaeologists call a "cultural dome"—a layer that was man-made. My son Jeremy and I participated in Jones's Spring 1998 dig at the mouth of this very cave.

Paleobotany tests confirmed that the reddish material found at the north entrance to the Cave of the Column was organic and traces of 9 spices were found. Tests by Dr. Terry Hutter (associated with Louisiana State University), palynological analyst, showed the presence of saffron, three kinds of cinnamon (*Cinnamomum verum* inner bark, *Cinnamomum vernum* outer bark and costus, which is new growth of the same *C. vernum* plant), balsam, myrrh, galbanum, cassia, frankincense, spikenard and onycha.

In Dr. Hutter's palynological analysis of the incense was this note about the spice spikenard:

> These flowers are small, violet to blue in color, and end with a terminal spike. . . Due to a thin husk, the spikenard is also the most difficult of the nine spices to grind to a fine consistency. It should also be noted that several complete flowers of the Spikenard were recovered intact in the 'spice' samples at Qumran. (Emphasis added.)[4]

The incense was carefully laid in a rock-like trough with 11 distinct layers covering them. Two other ingredients that Talmudic sources say were a part of the incense, Sodom salt and karsinia lye were found nearby in niches in the wall.

Dr. Hutter included in his report the following observations:

> The aroma released from the 'spices' during its processing was profuse and almost immediate. It initially saturated my hands as well as the clothes that I was wearing. Within a matter of minutes my laboratory and the surrounding area (for an area of several meters) was affected by the scent released from the 'spices.' . . . During the course of the week,

the odor lessened slightly but was still noticeable in and around my lab. Within a few weeks the distinct aroma of the spices diminished to a 'freshness or cleanness' of the air in my lab and the surrounding area. This aroma was in evidence, if even so slightly, for approximately two months. On days of high humidity the aroma would return with greater intensity."[5]

In the newspaper story I wrote on the incense (June 25, 1992) I noted: "The Mishnah tells how the priestly family of Avtinas possessed the secret of the preparation of the incense and that it was manufactured in quantities of 368 manehs (which authorities say was either 580 or 825 pounds) in a room situated in the upper story at the southern side of the Court of the Priests in the temple. The fragrance was so sweet that, the Mishnah records, 'from Jericho (12 miles) away they could smell the scent at the compounding of the incense.'" After reading Dr. Hutter's experience with igniting the incense in his laboratory, you can certainly imagine that the twice-daily burning of incense in the Jerusalem Temple would be noticeable throughout the Holy City.

In the May 23, 1992 International Jerusalem Post, Rabbi Menachem Burstin, who visited the Qumran dig after the incense was discovered, said: "In the Talmud it says that pilgrims coming from Jericho to Jerusalem could smell this mixture of the *shemen afarsimon* (anointing oil) and *pitum haketoret* (incense) and realized that their eyes would soon behold the temple itself."

The Israel Antiquities Department denied that what Jones found was incense and revoked his permit. For six years Jones would apply for permits only to be denied. He was able to dig in the first place because of the law of "status quo." Jones had been on the Stechool/Haas excavation team under a Jordanian permit when the Six Day War broke out. He was legally able to continue working in the Qumran area under that clause. In 1994, Israeli archaeologist Hanan Eschel and Magen Broshi, former director of the Shrine of the Book where the scrolls are stored, contacted Jones and asked to work with him, using some of his volunteers. They dug; he didn't.

But during those six years while Jones waited for his permit to be approved, he was busy with non-invasive archaeology to determine the location of Gilgal and a Solomonic copper mine and continuing to search out ancient sources.

Jones searched the Judean wasteland seeking the places mentioned in the Bible like I Kings 7:45-46:

> And the pots, and the shovels, and the basons: and all these vessels, which Hiram made to King Solomon for the house of the Lord, were of bright brass.
> In the plain of Jordan did the king cast them, in the clay ground between Succoth and Zarthan.

Because Jones could not dig during those years he was denied a permit, he gathered together a team of experts to help him locate Gilgal. This important site is where the Tabernacle was first set up when Joshua led the Children of Israel into the land following the death of Moses. Gilgal is where the Tabernacle stayed for 12 years.

The team that Jones organized included Arnon Karnieli from the Ben Gurion University - Sed Boker campus, Blaustein Institute of Desert Research Remote Sensing Laboratory and Ya'acov Arkin of the Israeli Institute of Geology. Also, Alex Beck and Amit Ronan from the Israel Government Petroleum, Geology and Geographics Institute. Jones arranged for flyover photography by Ofeq Arial Photography Limited, the company that does photography for the Israeli military. Jones used NASA satellite photos and Ground Penetrating Radar to discover the site of ancient Gilgal.

When Jones located a site in the Jordan Valley (far from where modern-day maps place Gilgal), his workers uncovered ancient three-foot high stone walls that surrounded the area where the Tabernacle stood.

This wall marked the area as holy and no one was to walk further unless they were purified. The wall had suffered breaches where workers from a nearby kibbutz had broken through with a bulldozer when they created a drainage ditch years ago. (And it touched me deeply that when Jones and his workers began uncovering the wall around where the Tabernacle may have stood, he instructed everyone to remove their shoes: for this was holy ground.)

Jones has found a truly biblical solution to the tremendous problem of what happens if he does find the Temple treasure, including the Ashes of the Red Heifer and the ancient Tabernacle. "To the Temple Mount!" would be the cry of Jewish faithful—and the Muslim response would be *jihad!*

But consider what it says in Amos 9:11-12:

> In that day I will raise up the tabernacle of David that is
> fallen, and close up the breaches thereof; and I will raise up
> his ruins, and I will build it as in the days of old: That they
> may possess the remnant of Edom, and of all the heathen,
> which are called by my name, saith the Lord that doeth this.

The "heathen" or gentiles who are called by the Lord's name will do this, not Jews. Very interesting says Jones! Israel has clear title to the land where Jones places biblical Gilgal. During the late 1800s, the Jewish people began purchasing land from the Sultan of Turkey to create a Jewish state—long before the Hashemite Kingdom of Transjordan was created by the British. Jones says that Gilgal was the first area bought and paid for with hard currency.

If Jones does find temple artifacts and the ancient Tabernacle, they could be placed at Gilgal. Israel would return to its first beginnings as Jones interprets the "at the first" and "at the beginning" of Isaiah 1:26, and no Muslim holy sites would be disturbed.

Temple Treasures: But Which Temple?

There is one very unique idea that Jones puts forth about the Copper Scroll—he believes it contains cryptic directions to locate Temple treasure and artifacts. It's just that he also believes the treasure is from the First Temple! There is a tradition in the Apocrypha that the Ark was hidden away by Jeremiah. In the Douay-Rheims Second Maccabees 2:5 it reads:

> And when Jeremias came thither he found a hollow cave: and he carried in thither the tabernacle and the ark and the altar of incense and so stopped the door.

We get a tantalizing clue the location of this cave from Second Kings 25:4-5 where it says that King Zedekiah tried to escape captivity "by way of a gate between the two walls, which is by the king's garden." The history recorded in Second Kings tells us "(now the Chaldees were against the city round about)" and "the army of the Chaldees pursued after the king and overtook him in the plains of Jericho." How did he manage to get clear to the Jericho area before being captured if he merely slipped through some gate? Remember, the Bible says the city was surrounded.

What if the gate led to a tunnel? One that runs from Jerusalem to the Valley of Achor near Jericho? Jones believes that the cavern where Jeremiah hid the Temple artifacts is the exit from the cave of Zedekiah which begins just north of the Damascus Gate.

He has done his homework and quotes from the three-volume scholarly edition of the Temple Scroll by Yigael Yadin. Yadin notes that *Pesiqta Rabbati* 26, ed. M. Ish-Shalom, page 131a says: "When Zedekiah saw this, he went out to flee in the cavern that led to Jericho, the place of the water conduit."[6] Jones maintains that the cavern descends toward the Dead Sea and exits in the Valley of Achor—where the Cave of the Column is located. Just after my son and I left Israel, Jones took the other volunteers beneath the streets of Jerusalem to the walled-up beginning of Zedekiah's Cave, a claustrophobia-inducing trip few tourists get to take.

Now that we are placed historically prior to the destruction of the first Temple, we can explore Jones' theory. He writes: "The Copper Scroll, contrary to popular belief, deals primarily with the treasures of the ancient Tabernacle, not the Herodian Temple! Except for the spices of the incense (*Qetoret*) and the Ashes of the Red Heifer (that are contained within a vessel called the '*Kalal*'), the items that are described in the Copper Scroll all belong to the First Commonwealth, not the Second. That also would explain why two things from the First Temple were not present in the Second Temple (i.e., the Ark of the Covenant and the *Shemen Afarsimon* (Anointing Oil)."[7]

There is also the matter of a book published in Amsterdam in 1648 C.E. by Rabbi Naftali (ben Elchanan) Hertz that discusses the Copper Scroll. Jones wrote in one of his newsletters that the rabbi "cites as his source an almost forgotten addition or *Tosefta* to the Talmud in Mishnah III under the section of *Qillim* [vessels]." Jones noted that some scholars had failed to find any mention of a Copper Scroll in this *Tosefta* in modern copies.

But the *Tosefta* found in the Cairo *Geniza* in 1896 by Solomon Schecter verifies Rabbi Hertz's book. [There is a wonderful explanation of why Jews stored old books and manuscripts like in the Cairo *Geniza*. In *The Torah: A Modern Commentary*, the editors write: "Every parchment or paper, religious or secular, on which the name of God had been inscribed was preserved and, when no longer in use, 'hidden away' in storage (hence the name '*Genizah*,' from *ganaz*, to hide."] This *Geniza* in Cairo also had priceless copies of the Damascus Document later found among the Dead Sea Scrolls. The *Tosefta* found in the Cairo *Geniza*, says Jones, mentioned a "silver chest containing the garments of the High Priest, the Breastplate, the Ephod and the Urim and Thummim."

In his book Rabbi Hertz entitled a selection "*Emeq HaMelekh*" or "Valley of the King." Jones quotes the following from Hertz's Mishnah 2 of "*Emeq HaMelekh*": "These are the holy vessels and the vessels of the

Temple that were in Jerusalem and in every place. They were inscribed by Shimur HaLevi and his companions, on a 'Luach Nehoshet' [Copper Plate], with all the Vessels of the Holy of Holies that Shlomo son of David made. And together with Shimur were Hizkiyahu [Hezekiah], Zidkiyah [Zedekiah], Haggai the Prophet and Zechariah, son of Berachiah, son of Ido the Prophet." Jones also notes that in the same year the Copper Scroll was found, two marble tablets signed by "the servant of HaShem, Shimur HaLevi" were found in a basement storage room of a museum in Beirut, Lebanon. Like the Copper Scroll, the marble tablets were written in *bas relief*, which means that the letters stood out from the surface they were chiseled on. (Jones has said that the Copper Scroll was written or punched out from the backside which made the letters protrude forward.) Jones firmly believes that the Copper Scroll is the *Luach Nehoshet* that was written by these five men and hidden in the Qumran Cave. His evidence seems to support this claim.

Jones says that the "exit" door he will uncover at the Cave of the Column is more than 23 feet high and 66 feet wide—larger than the overpass of a three-lane freeway. He also believes that this is the "door of hope" for Israel spoken of in Hosea 2:15:

> And I will give her vineyards from thence, and the valley
> of Achor for a door of hope: and she shall sing there as in
> the day when she came up out of the land of Egypt.

Isaiah 65:10 also has comforting words to say concerning this valley that was barren and bleak:

> And Sharon shall be a fold of flocks, and the valley of
> Achor a place for the herds to lie down in, for my people
> that have sought me.

*Volunteers man the buckets
on the 1998 excavation*

As I stood overlooking the Valley of Achor from the north entrance of the Cave of the Column in April 1998, I saw acres and acres of vineyards in the desolate land the Jews have reclaimed from the desert. I certainly believe that God has a door waiting to be opened. For if Jones does find the Ashes, the Tabernacle and the Ark of the Covenant—then Malachi's words could be fulfilled:

Then shall the offering of Judah and Jerusalem be pleasant unto the Lord, as in the days of old, and as in former years. Malachi 3:4.

What is the Significance of the Word "*Kalal*"?

In 1997 I had the opportunity to interview several scholars on the International Dead Sea Scrolls team. I asked each a question about a word Vendyl Jones found in the Copper Scroll and one that makes Jones's work significant. "What does *kalal* mean?"

Two local rabbis had previously said kalal is a generic word for "pitcher" and nothing more. And that's what Shmaryahu Talmon, a Dead Sea Scroll expert, said as well.

I have in my library six different translations of the Copper Scroll. Jones's translation leaves the word in Hebrew to make note of its uniqueness. And of the other five, Florentino Garcia Martinez translates *kalal* as "an amphora;" Wise, Abegg and Cook say "an urn" and Geza Vermes, Al Wolters and John Marco Allegro say "pitcher." But only Jones and Allegro tie the word to its Mishnaic use—as the vessel that held the Ashes of the Red Heifer.

In Allegro's book on the Copper Scroll he writes: "It was through the eastern gate that the High Priest and his party went forth to the Mount of Olives during the ceremony of the burning of the Red Heifer (Nu 19:2). Interestingly enough, the word used by our scribe for 'pitcher' [*kalal*] coincides with that found in rabbinic tradition for the vessel containing the ashes of the sacrifice."[8]

In Mishnah Parah 3, 3, the word *kalal* is used twice with this footnote: "It was a special vessel in which were kept the ashes of all the red heifers from the time of Moses onwards." In other places where the sages spoke of vessels in which spring water was placed and then some of the ashes of the heifer to make the water of purification, a number of other words are used, not *kalal*. In most places the word is *keli*. Other Hebrew terms are used for the words "bottle," "urn" or "flask." Only when the rabbis intend the meaning to be the special vessel in which all the ashes were stored (prior to use in the Temple by the priests for Yom Kippur or sacrificing another Red Heifer) do they use the word *kalal*.

In Hershel Shanks, *Understanding the Dead Sea Scrolls*, published in 1992, an article by P. Kyle McCarter cited reasons why scholars are beginning to believe the Copper Scroll just might be for real. (It took 33 years and four editions before Scroll scholar Geza Vermes included the Copper Scroll in his *The Dead Sea Scrolls in English*.) McCarter wrote that most treasure folklore claimed to show the hiding places of Temple treasure and sacred vessels and usually would refer to Jeremiah or Moses. But, McCarter says, the Copper Scroll "is plodding and businesslike. Neither Moses nor Jeremiah is there, nor is any famous relic—neither the Ark <u>nor the ashes of the red heifer</u>."[9] (Emphasis added.)

One wonders why McCarter ignores the word *kalal* found in the Copper Scroll, and the anointing oil and incense found at Qumran almost next-door to the cave where the Copper Scroll was found. Every day when we hiked up the hill to the north entrance to the Cave of the Column on Jones' dig, we passed by the small cave where the Copper Scroll was found.

The vial of oil discovered on the 1988 dig has been tested extensively and discovered to be balsam oil. This exceedingly precious oil came from the area of Ein Gedi. These balsam plants were uprooted by Titus and taken back to Rome, where it was found that they only would grow below sea level. The Talmud records that in the days of Josiah, the anointing oil was hidden so balsam was the oil used from then on to anoint kings (Ker. 5b; TJ, Sot. 8:1; 22c).

But no one in academia gives Jones the slightest bit of credit for this significant find. On Jones's 1998 dig at Qumran in April his media specialist and photographer, Jim Long, told me that Hershel Shanks, editor of *Biblical Archaeology Review*, had contacted Vendyl's office for information. Shanks told Long he was doing a new book on the scrolls and couldn't do a chapter on the Copper Scroll without input from Vendyl. Long quickly sent photos and reports on the digs. Yet when the book, *The Mystery and Meaning of the Dead Sea Scrolls*, came out in early 1998 there was not one word about Jones or his discoveries. Long questioned Shanks as to why and was told that the publisher didn't want it in the book.

Historian and author Neil Asher Silberman is one who views the Copper Scroll as a document with religious significance. He writes:

> The author [of the Copper Scroll] was well acquainted with the villages and towns of Judea, with the tombs and complex system of watercourses that ran through them that had long been the province of Jerusalem priests. More than that, the author used the technical terminology of tithes, consecrated vessels and offerings that were part of the complex balance of national obligations and economic independence that the Temple stood for.[10]

Ashes needed for the Red Heifer Sacrifice and Yom Kippur

One intriguing detail in the Sacrifice of the Red Heifer is the fact that prior to officiating in the ritual, the priest (and traditionally it was the High Priest in all instances after Eliezer) was isolated in a stone chamber in the Temple for the week before the ceremony. The only other time this was done was the week prior to Yom Kippur. The Red Heifer sacrifice seems to have had a special significance to be so tied with Yom Kippur.

During this week before he sacrificed the Red Heifer, the High Priest was sprinkled with water mingled with ashes each of those seven days. In the week before Yom Kippur the rabbis believe the High Priest was sprinkled only on the third and seventh days.[11] Being in a stone chamber made it impossible for the priest to contract uncleanliness.

It seems that in order to sacrifice a new heifer, the priest must be sprinkled with the ashes of the previous heifers. While Rabbi Richman advocates another way to have a pure priest, finding Red Heifer ashes that have been sequestered for almost 2,000 years would solve a lot of problems—if the vessel was not rendered unclean in the process of discovery. Jones was asked years ago by then-Chief Rabbi of Israel, Shlomo Goren, "what would you do if you found the *kalal?*" "Nothing," said Jones, "we must not touch it." "Exactly right!" said Rabbi Goren.

Jones believes the ashes are inside a vessel made of clay and the dung of the heifer as described in the Mishnah. He says this clay vessel is kept inside a bronze (or copper) vessel. The outer vessel has eyelets around the rim and the procedure for moving it would be weaving hyssop through the eyelets, inserting two poles through the hyssop and having ten boys under the age of Bar Mitzvah carry the vessel to Jerusalem.

The closest I have come to verifying Jones's statement that the outer vessel is copper, is that this suggestion may come from Ben-Zion Luria, who wrote a book on the Copper Scroll in 1963, *The Copper Scroll from the Desert of Judeah.* Unfortunately, the book is long out of print and copies that are available are written in Hebrew which I can only read haltingly. (Would someone like to support my getting a degree in Hebrew?!) So I haven't been able to validate Jones's assertion at this time. But apparently Luria was not so quick to dismiss the Copper Scroll. Jones uses this quote from Luria's introduction to his book that ". . .the [Copper] scroll can not be understood without a knowledge of rabbinic literature and vocabulary" and "the validity and authenticity of the Copper Scroll will remain in question until one single item mentioned in the scroll is discovered. Once something is found at Qumran that is listed among the 64 designated items and places, the scroll's validity will be unquestioned."[12]

Will Vendyl Jones uncover a hidden chamber at the Cave of the Column and find the Ashes of the Red Heifer and the other Temple artifacts? I certainly can't predict this. But Jones was able to fund yet another drill exploration of the site. He attempted to drill four or five 4-inch holes in which a miniature camera (with infra-red capabilities) was to be inserted to check for the cavern Jones believes is there. The drill, however, was unable to penetrate the loose rock from previous excavations. So Vendyl Jones waits for another opportunity to resume his work at the Cave of the Column. Should Jones one day succeed in finding lost treasures of the Temple, the implications are simply staggering.

"He Was Despised and We Esteemed Him Not"

There is one last thing to ponder since I would like to add an interpretive gleaning of my own. I have searched Young's *Analytical Concordance to the Bible* and Wilson's *Old Testament Word Studies* (page 545) for uses of the word *kalal.* I find the results intriguing.

Most often *kalal* is used for the word "curse" (39 times). It also can mean to be despised, to be lightly esteemed, to be a light thing, to bring into contempt. Then there are the times when it is used to mean to lighten or make lighter, to be easier, to set light (by one) and as an adjective to describe brass: "polished" and "burnished." It seems as though this one Hebrew word has some pretty contradictory meanings!

But it makes perfect sense to me for the rabbis to call the vessel that held the remnant ashes of all Red Heifers a *kalal,* because those ashes represent both the curse of death and sin (twice in Numbers 19 the words "purification for sin" are used) and the way to remove it. Certainly the ashes purify and yet make the priest impure at the same time!

In Deuteronomy 21:23 we are told "he that is hanged is accursed of God" and the word for accursed is *kalallah*, a feminine form of *kalal*. The New Testament tells us that Christ was made sin for us (2 Cor. 5:21) which was symbolized by His "hanging on a tree"—the wooden cross of Golgotha.

Rev. F. B. Myer remarked on this theme of the curse: "ROYALTY THROUGH THORNS—It is very remarkable that the sign of the curse became on the brow of Christ, the insignia of royalty. The lesson is obvious—that he has transformed the curse into a blessing: that he has discovered the secret of compelling it to yield to royalty."[13] (Emphasis in original.)

Is this not what the Ashes of the Red Heifer do as well? To transform the curse of death (with its accompanying uncleanliness) into life—a life now sanctified and permitted to tread upon holy ground.

Another "type" for this duality (the very symbol of sin and at the same time the cure) was the serpent made of brass (actually copper as Wilson's Old Testament Word Studies says on page 49: "brass, brasen; copper seems frequently intended, when translated brass, and may therefore be the proper meaning of the word.") All who were dying of the bite of the fiery serpents in Numbers 21 had only to look up at the serpent on the pole to be saved. We also must look to the One who was made sin for us in order to be cleansed from our own sins. He makes our burdens light, He takes away the curse by having *become* it and thus makes us bright and clean. He is the Light sent to guide us through this wilderness of life.

But there is yet another meaning for the word "*kalal.*" In Ezekiel's vision of the four living creatures, he wrote that "the sole of their feet was like the sole of a calf's foot: and they sparkled like the colour of burnished <u>brass</u>" Ezekiel 1:7 (emphasis added). The word for burnished is *kalal.* The only other similar use is in Daniel 10:6 where Daniel sees a glorious vision of a Man, whom Matthew Henry said "could be no other than Christ himself, the eternal Word."[14] Daniel writes: ". . . and his arms and feet like in colour to <u>polished</u> brass" (emphasis added). Yes, the word for polished is "*kalal.*"

It is my understanding that uses of the word "brass" have to do with judgment. John saw a similar vision in Revelation 1:15 where he described seeing Christ: "And his feet like unto fine brass, as if they burned in a furnace." The fact that Christ's feet are like polished brass fits in with the symbolism of judgment: "For he must reign, till he hath put all enemies under his feet," (1 Cor. 15:25).

The apocalyptic visions of the End Times include Christ treading the wicked under His feet in a great winepress. Revelation 14:19-20 tells us how the wicked of the earth are gathered for judgment: "And the angel thrust in his sickle into the earth, and gathered the vine of the earth, and cast it into the great winepress of the wrath of God. And the winepress was trodden without the city, and blood came out of the winepress, even unto the horse bridles, by the space of a thousand and six hundred furlongs."

In Revelation 19:13, 15, Christ "is clothed with a vesture dipped in blood; and his name is called the Word of God. . . and he treadeth the winepress of the fierceness and wrath of Almighty God."

And think of the promise of Genesis 3:15 that while the serpent may crush the heel of the Seed of the Woman, He (Christ, the Seed of the Woman) would crush the serpent's head! (Keil and Delitzsch, write that the Hebrew word translated "bruise"in the King James Version is better translated "crush" per Chaldee, Syriac and Rabbinical authorities. They write:

> However pernicious may be the bite of a serpent in the heel when the poison circulates throughout the body it is not immediately fatal and utterly incurable like the crushing of the serpent's head.[15]

I suggest that if Vendyl Jones finds the Ashes of the Red Heifer, it may have just as much significance for Christians as it does for Jews. For have we not been cleansed by the sprinkling of Christ's blood? As David, we have all at one time (or many times) prayed to be purged from our sins. May we all look to the One who has power to cleanse us and keep us bright!

1. Al Wolters, *The Copper Scroll: Overview, Text and Translation,* Sheffield Academic Press, 1996, Sheffield, England, page 12.

2. Quoted in *The Mystery and Meaning of the Dead Sea Scrolls,* Hershel Shanks, Random House, 1998, page 186.

3. *A Brief Biography of Vendyl Jones: Digging Up the Future,* published by Jones' Institute of Judaic-Christian Research, nd, page 3.

4. Vendyl Jones, *The Copper Scroll and Excavations at Qumran,* in consortium with Louisiana State University and Hebrew University, Compiled by Professor Vendyl Jones, Vendyl Jones Research Institutes, Inc., 1993, page 60.

5. Ibid, page 53.

6. *The Temple Scroll,* edited by Yigael Yadin, The Israel Exploration Society, The Institute of Archaeology of the Hebrew University of Jersualem, The Shrine of the Book, Jerusalem, 1983, Vol. 1, page 224.

7. *Qumran Excavations,* Vendyl Jones, page 8.

8. John Marco Allegro, *The Treasures of the Copper Scroll,* Second Revised Edition, Garden City, NY, Doubleday, page 104.

9. Hershel Shanks, *Understanding the Dead Sea Scrolls,* Random House, NY, 1992, page 237.

10. Niel Asher Silberman, *The Hidden Scrolls,* Riverhead Books, New York, 1994, page 140.

11. *Parah Adumah,* Mishnah 3, 1, Vol. 6, Judaica Press, Gateshead, England, 1983, page 414

12. Quoted in *Qumran Excavations: Cave of the Column Complex and Environs,* Vendyl Jones, page 3.

13. Rev. F.B. Meyer, *Expositions of Isaiah XL-LV: Christ in Isaiah,* Fleming H. Revell Company, New York, 1895, pages 238-239.

14. Matthew Henry, *Complete and Unabridged Matthew Henry's Commentary on the Whole Bible,* Hendrickson Publishers, 1992, page 1455.

15. C.F. Keil and F. Delitzch, *Commentary on the Old Testament in Ten Volumes,* Wm. B. Eerdmans Publishing Company, 1985, Vol. 1, page 100.

Chapter Six

"Though Your Sins Be As Scarlet"
The Crimson Metaphor

From Bozrah
by Lori Fiechter
(Used with permission)

Wool and scarlet
Milk and Wine;
Garments sin-stained,
Black with grime.
Armies march
In linens bright:
Washed in Blood,
Made snowy white.
See their Captain,
King and Lord
Brandishing His
Mighty sword!

Once He suffered,
Pressed as wine
He has come to rule
this time!
He marches forth
And who can stand?
The Cup of Wrath
Is in His hand.
The Day of Vengeance
Is proclaimed
From Bozrah to
Meggido's plain.

On the gentle slopes of the Mount of Olives, the Sacrifice of the Red Heifer was carried out. Through this biblical ritual a first-born, never-yoked, pure-red heifer is turned to white ash. *Red to white.* Is it possible that Isaiah pondered this thing? Could this sacrifice be a metaphor we haven't understood until now?

The following verse in Isaiah mentioned things that are red and white, but in a context that was utterly mystifying to me: "Ho, every one that thirsteth, come ye to the waters, and he that hath no money, come ye, buy and eat; yea, come, <u>buy wine and milk</u>, without money and without price." Isaiah 55:1. (Emphasis added.) I understand that Isaiah was inviting all to come to the *Waters of Salvation*, to Jesus Christ, the Living Water. This invitation is echoed beautifully in the NIV's rendition of Rev. 22:17:

> Whoever is thirsty, let him come; and whoever wishes, let him take the free gift of the water of life.

But Isaiah's wine and milk reference made no sense to me at all. And yet, I couldn't simply dismiss the part I didn't understand. This verse would not leave me alone! And it seemed that red-and-white imagery was the key to deciphering these mysterious words. I focused on red and white because in biblical times wine was called "the blood of grapes," (Deut. 32:14) or red—and milk was obviously white. One reference work I consulted said, "From the designation of the juice of the grapes as their 'blood,' it may be concluded that red grapes were mostly highly prized. This is confirmed by the use of the term *soreq* ('red,' Isaiah 5:2, Jeremiah 2:21) for the vines of the best quality ('the choicest vine'), which indicates that they were so called from their red grapes."[1] Just to add one more reference, from the Mishnah and the explanatory note for it: "They may not bring old wine [more than twelve months—the rich red colour has faded]."[2]

There was simply no "resonance" with any other way of looking at these two words except by their color.

I have learned to pay attention to verses of scripture that linger in my head and heart. This was one of those intriguing passages that reverberated with deeper meanings to be sought out. To come to understand it, I applied one of the sweetest biblical lessons I ever learned: Simply put, truths are scattered like puzzle pieces in a seemingly random fashion throughout Holy Writ. Whenever one verse reminds me of another, or uses the same wording, no matter how far apart in the Bible, I make the connection, compare the verses and pay attention to what the Holy Spirit is trying to teach me. It is amazing how often the Word of God interprets itself if one just has the patience to inquire of the Lord and to seek a connection among His scriptures. In fact, it is almost a commandment! Remember this scripture quoted in the introduction:

> Call unto me, and I will answer thee, and show thee great
> and mighty things which thou knowest not. Jeremiah 33:3

One such connection was in Daniel 12:10 where he tells us, "Many shall be purified and made white..." I knew that Rev. 7:14 teaches that those who come out of the Tribulation "have washed their robes, and made them white in the blood of the Lamb." And Psalm 51:7 beautifully tells us, "wash me and I shall be whiter than snow." White obviously signifies a redeemed state.

Red seems to have multiple meanings. As it is the color of blood, it can represent life: "For the life of the flesh is in the blood: and I have given it to you upon the altar to make an atonement for your souls: for it is the blood that maketh an atonement for the soul," Leviticus 17:11.

But it is most often representative of man's sinful state. The definitive scripture tying sin to the color red is found in Isaiah 1:18: "though your sins be as scarlet . . ."

In *The Book of Our Heritage*, by Jewish educator Eliyahu Kitov, he writes that in the second year after Israel had departed from Egypt, they were all made to undergo purification with the Ashes of the Red Heifer:

... all Israel was required to undergo the purification of 'the red heifer,' regardless of their defilement through contact with the dead or not, since they had all been involved in the sin of the golden calf; and idolatry defiles like the dead. After God was reconciled with Israel, and commanded them to build the Mishkan [Tabernacle] for him, so that He might dwell in their midst, He gave them this mitzvah [the Red Heifer] as a means of purification from all defilement; whether that of contact with the dead, or that of idolatry (which is the root of all death in the world).[3]

In *The Zohar* it says: "The word 'scarlet' may also be taken to indicate the robes of judgement, which is assumed for the punishment of idolators. For one day God will put on a red robe and take a red sword to take vengeance on the ruddy one [Esau]. This we learn from the verse: 'Who is this that cometh from Edom with dyed garments, etc.' "[4] (You will be reading a lot more about that connection with Isaiah 63!) But again, we must look to the context in which symbols are used.

Solving the enigma of the "come to the waters" wine-and-milk passage was truly opened up when I turned to the prophet who wrote these words. I was drawn back time and time again to Isaiah 1:18: "Come now, and let us reason together, saith the Lord: though your sins be as scarlet, they shall be white as snow; though they be red like crimson, they shall be as wool."

It is plain that Isaiah is calling all Israel (and that means all of mankind) to rid themselves of their scarlet sin and to become purified. To do that we must come to the Waters of Salvation and drink. The only Way, is to come to Jesus Christ, the Living Water—to drink deeply of that water that will never run out and will quench every thirst eternally. To that water which can spring up out of our very hearts. We are "well" acquainted with the image of Christ as Living Water and about drinking this water that will never run dry. Isaiah tells us to come to the water and receive it FREE, without money or price. We can't buy or earn this salvation, it comes through the beautiful grace of Jesus Christ on condition of our sincere repentance. We must bow our knees and our hearts to proclaim that Jesus is the Christ and that through Him we can claim the covering of His blood so that we may be forgiven. And then we must show our love for Him by keeping His commandments and serving Him.

But after Isaiah directed us to come to the Living Water of Jesus Christ, he said for us to buy *wine and milk* without money or price. Somehow this Water is connected with wine and milk. It seemed that I was close to understanding this now but I wondered if these two words had puzzled anyone else?

The Christian View

In Matthew Henry's *Commentary on the Whole Bible* comes the following remarks about this passage:

> "Observe: (1) Who are invited: Ho, every one. Not the Jews only, to whom first the word of salvation was sent, but the Gentiles, the poor, the maimed, the halt and the blind, are called to this marriage supper, whoever can be picked up out of the highways and the hedges. . . (2) What is the qualification required in those that shall be welcome - they must thirst....Where God gives grace he first gives a thirsting after it; and, where he has given a thirsting after it, he will give it, Ps. 81:10. . .(3) Whither they are invited: Come you to the waters. . .Come to Christ; for he is the fountain opened; he is the rock smitten. . . (4) What they are invited to do —come, and buy . . . make it your own by an appointment of the grace of the gospel to yourselves . . . (5) What is the provision they are invited to: 'Come and buy wine and milk, which will not only quench the thirst' (fair water would do that), 'but nourish the body and revive the spirits.' . . . We come to the waters, and would

be glad of them, but we find there wine and milk, which were the staple commodities of the tribe of Judah, and which the Shiloh of that tribe is furnished with to entertain the gathering of the people to him, Gen. 49:10, 12. 'His eyes shall be red with wine and his teeth white with milk.' We must come to Christ, to have milk for babes, to nourish and cherish those that are but lately born again; and with him strong men shall find that which will be a cordial to them: they shall have wine to make glad their hearts. We must part with our puddle-water, nay with our poison, that we may procure this wine and milk."[5]

Henry notes that the waters of this verse refer to Christ (the rock smitten) and he refers to the "Shiloh" prophecy of Genesis 49:12, rightly attributing to Shiloh the equally enigmatic phrase about Shiloh's eyes being red with wine and his teeth white with milk. But when he gets to the part about the wine and milk, he moves away from continuing the water of salvation theme. He is not alone. Others suggest these symbols refer to the 'wine of joy' and the 'milk of richness.'

In Adam Clarke's commentary on these verses in Isaiah, he quotes the Jewish Rabbi David Kimchi (c. 1220) and then adds his own beliefs about this verse:

"Water," says Kimchi, "is a metaphor for the law and wisdom: as the world cannot subsist without water, so it is impossible that it can subsist without wisdom." The law is also compared to wine and milk: to wine because wine rejoiceth the heart, as it is written: "The statutes of the Lord are right, rejoicing the heart," Psalm 19:8. It is compared also to milk, because milk is the subsistence of the child; so are the words of the law the nourishment of his soul who walks in the Divine teaching, and grows up under it.[6]

These suggestions by commentators whose word I honor have much food for thought in them. But I believe there is more to be gleaned from Isaiah's metaphor.

The Crimson Metaphor

My *pesher* or explanation of this verse would be to suggest that this wine-and-milk imagery teaches us just *what it is* that coming to the Water will do for us: **to change our red, sin-laden robes to pure white through the "sure mercies of David"—Jesus Christ, the beloved Son of God.** In other words, come to the Living Water of Jesus Christ where you can be washed and made clean, where through His grace, your scarlet robes become pure white through His shed blood. I believe Isaiah intended for us to understand that his two commentaries on red-to-white (Isaiah 55:1 and 1:18) need to be read in tandem to receive the complete message.

When I came to understand that Isaiah was telling us that the Water of Salvation (Jesus Christ and His blessed Atonement) create the miracle that can turn red to white and then searched many Christian reference works, I thought that perhaps I had come up with an original exegesis of this verse. But a careful perusal of Jewish sources showed me that wise Jewish commentators made this connection millennia ago (although it is my belief that they still need to learn the real identity of their *Moshiach*). Following are a number of these references that taught about Isaiah's red-to-white metaphor and said more to me about the Messiah than many of the Christian commentaries!

Jewish Exegesis of 'Red to White'

How beautiful and complete God's Word is! The more you study it, the more it amazes and intrigues you. Will it surprise you to find out that Isaiah's red-to-white metaphor is expounded upon in Jewish writings about Yom Kippur, the Day of Atonement? And isn't that exactly where a picture of cleansing red to white should be found? Atonement! The very act that "covers" our sins through the blood of Christ.

I owe so much gratitude to those faithful Jews who protected and preserved Jewish writings like the Mishnah, Talmud, Aggadah and mystical works like *The Zohar, The Bahir* and *Sefer Yetzirah*, through the long centuries of Christian persecution. How many treasures were lost through the hate-filled years of pogroms and Crusades and Inquisitions with their murder, torture and book-burnings.

I have come to recognize the beauty and worth of the original olive tree which I am grafted into through the Holy One of Israel! (See Romans 11:17-18.) You may find it odd that a devout Christian would love these ancient Jewish writings, but some of the sweetest Messianic insights I have found anywhere come from these sources.

The author of *The Life and Times of Jesus the Messiah*, Alfred Edersheim, made a similar observation:

> Much that is found in Cabbalistic writings approximates so closely to the higher truths of Christianity, that, despite the errors, superstitions, and foibles that mingle with it, we cannot fail to recognize the continuance and the remains of those deeper facts of Divine revelation, which must have formed the substance of prophetic teaching under the Old Testament, and have been understood, or at least hoped for, by those who were under the guidance of the Holy Spirit.[7]

It is important to remember that both Christians and Jews love God and are waiting for *Moshiach*. I believe we are using different names and rituals in worshiping the same God. Both religions think that the other needs to be "straightened out" as to who the Messiah really is. I loved what Gershon Salomon (head of Temple Mount Faithful) told a group of Evangelical Christians in Jerusalem in 1992 when he said, "We'll wait until He gets here and then ask Him if it's His first or second visit!"

I hope I am never so small-minded that I will overlook the deep insights of righteous Jews. I also hope you will forgive me this small divergence. I have interviewed too many Holocaust survivors and Righteous Gentiles to not take a moment to abhor the disgraceful chapters of Christianity that brought shame to the name of the Jewish rabbi from Nazareth who came to the world to offer the precious gift of salvation.

And I wonder if we Christians have become so estranged from our Jewish roots to the point that we miss some of the incredible insights that God meant for us to discover in our study?

I am indebted to the work of David H. Stern whose *Jewish New Testament Commentary* has been a wonderful guide in my studies. This book has helped teach me how to think as symbolically as Isaiah wrote to understand how to decipher "types and shadows." In Stern's *Restoring the Jewishness of the Gospel,* he writes,

> The Messiah's vicarious atonement is rooted in the Jewish sacrificial system; the Lord's Supper is rooted in the Jewish Passover traditions; baptism is a Jewish practice; and indeed the entire New Testament is built on the Hebrew Bible with its prophecies and its promise of a New Covenant, so that the New Testament without the Old is as impossible as the second floor of a house without the first."[8]

The High Holy Days

Yom Kippur was (and of course, still is) the highest, holy day of Judaism. On that day, in addition to the regular sacrifices, two goats were chosen by drawing "lots." A lottery box has been recreated by the Temple Institute in Jerusalem. It is made of wood and gold and contains two lots, one marked "To the Lord" and the other marked "To *Azazel*" which the Institute calls "that place in the desert to which the Yom Kippur scapegoat was taken, carrying away the sins of Israel. By drawing lots, the High Priest decided which of two goats would remain in the Temple and which would be sent to the desert."[9]

As the High Priest reached into the box with both of his hands to pick out the lots, it was considered auspicious if the lot for the Lord came up in his right hand while the lot for *Azazel* came up in the left. (We all want to be on the right-hand of God and to avoid being sent to the left with the "goats"!)

There are many books that can shed light on this day and its many rituals. It is important to study Yom Kippur for the types and shadows that foretell the great sacrifice of Christ in His all-encompassing atonement which fulfilled this law of sacrifice. And we will find Isaiah's red-to-white metaphor over and over again in Jewish writings on Yom Kippur.

My favorite Yom Kippur book was found at the Temple Institute bookstore in Jerusalem, *The Abarbanel on the Yom Kippur Service in the Beis HaMikdash.* (Rabbi Yitzchak Abarbanel was born in Portugal in 1437 of royal lineage—he could trace his Sephardic family back to King David. While he was writing learned commentaries on biblical and prophetic subjects he also served as treasurer for a king and queen you may have heard of: King Ferdinand and Queen Isabella. Following their infamous expulsion of Spain's Jews in 1492, he went into exile in Italy where he completed his study of Deuteronomy and wrote a Torah commentary.)

From Abarbanel's book and references in the Mishnah and Talmud, I will focus on a trio of examples of the "Scarlet Metaphor." There are at least three instances of "red-to-white" imagery regarding atonement in the Yom Kippur ritual.

The Scarlet "Tongue"

Scarlet wool or thread (*lashon zehurit*) was tied to (1) the door of the sanctuary, (2) to the horns of the scapegoat and (3) to a chain or rope around the leg of the High Priest when he entered the Holy of Holies in the Temple—all on this holy

Scarlet wool displayed among Temple implements at the Temple Institute

day. The scarlet wool was visible proof that the sins of Israel had been atoned for—when it miraculously turned white.

From the Adin Steinsaltz translation of the Talmud comes this description of the Hebrew words *lashon zehurit*:

> Lit. a strip of crimson. A tongue-shaped strip of wool dyed with a special crimson dye (*tola'at shani*). A strip of this wool was employed in the performance of several mitzvot: (1) The sacrifice of the Red Heifer (*Parah Adumah*, Numbers 19:6.) (2) The purification ritual of a person previously afflicted with leprosy (Leviticus 14:4-6). (3) The Yom Kippur offerings. It was customary to tie such a crimson strip around the neck of the goat offered as a sin-offering and between the horns of the goat sent to Azazel.[10]

Midrash Rabbah on Deuteronomy connects the word "tongue" used to describe the scarlet wool with healing.

> The Holy One, blessed be He, said: 'See how beloved is the language of the Torah; it is healing for the tongue. Whence do we know this? For so Scripture says: "soothing [lit. 'healing'] tongue is a tree of life (Prov. 15:4); and 'tree of life' is but another term for Torah, as it is written, She is a tree of life to them that lay hold upon her (Prov. 3:18).[11]

When so many different words could have been used to describe this piece of scarlet wool, "thread," "line," "cord;" I find it very significant that the Oral Tradition notes that "tongue" is the word used here. This red wool would indeed bring healing as it was the means by which Israel would know if sin had been forgiven that year. (The "tongue" would tell!)

Day of Atonement: The Yom Kippur Service

The special service for atonement and forgiveness is described in Abarbanel's commentary where he writes there were two goats "for a sin offering, belonging communally to the nation, one of which was sacrificed and one of which was sent to Azazel, the wilderness." Before the scapegoat (and that's just exactly where this term came from) was sent out to die (carrying the sins of Israel), scarlet wool was tied to the goat's horns and also to the door of the sanctuary. Abarbanel writes of this scarlet wool tied to the goat's head and notes that rather than the door of the sanctuary, the wool was tied to the temple gate from which the goat is sent out. Regardless of which door or gate it was on, this scarlet wool was key to Israel knowing if their sins had been forgiven them for that year.

In the Mishnah (Yoma 6, 8) it says:

> They said to him—to the High Priest—"The he-goat has reached the wilderness." And whence did they know that the he-goat had arrived at the wilderness?—They used to set up sentry stations and wave with cloths, and thus they knew that the he-goat had reached the wilderness. . . R. Ishmael says, "And did they not have another sign?—A strip of crimson wool was tied to the door of the sanctuary and when the he-goat reached the wilderness [and was killed] the strip turned white; as it is said, 'Though your sins be as scarlet, they shall be as white as the snow.' "

In *The Shocken Book of Mystical Testimonies* a selection from *The Zohar* tells about a chain with scarlet thread wound through it which was attached to the High Priest: "Rabbi Isaac said: A chain was tied to the leg of the Priest as he went in so that if he died there they could pull his body out." Remember, no one except the High Priest was allowed to enter the Holy of Holies, even to remove the body of the current High Priest should he be stricken dead there.

It was no small thing to approach the Lord in the Holy of Holies if you were not worthy. What would happen to the man who had "purchased" the office of High Priest for wealth and prestige? Rabbi Judah Nadich notes that the high priests who served in the First Temple period were righteous so there were only 18 to hold this office. But during the time of the Second Temple wealthy men bribed their way into office so there were many more who held this position—Nadich estimates between 80 and 85. After deducting 141 years of service for four righteous High Priests (about 35 years each, a number fitting for what was supposed to be a lifetime position), Nadich suggests

> . . . it can be seen that none of the rest completed even one year of service. This was because they rose to the office not through merit but through bribery. For example, Martha, the daughter of Boethus[12], brought a measure full of dinars to King Alexander Yannai to persuade him to nominate her husband Joshua ben Gamla, for the high priesthood.[13]

And Abarbanel notes: "Many unworthy Kohanim met their death by the hands of Heaven in the Holy of Holies."[14] The priests officiating in the Temple had every right to suspect that their High Priest might have been killed if he tarried too long after entering the Holiest Place! And now that you know that the office of High Priest, which was supposed to be a lifetime job, was rolled over to the highest bidder, can't you detect a wee note of sarcasm in John's remark about Caiaphas being the high priest 'that year'?!

"How could they know? [continues the *Zohar* account about knowing if the High Priest died in the Holy of Holies] They knew it by means of the scarlet thread. For if its color did not change they would know that the Priest had remained there in the state of sin. But if he was to emerge in safety they would know it because then the colored thread would turn white. When that happened there was rejoicing both on high and below, otherwise they were all distressed and all would know that their prayers had gone unanswered."[15]

The commentary that follows this selection notes: "Red is the color of judgment, white the color of mercy. The thread turning white symbolized the harmony and grace that reigns on this day on high so that in the realm of the *Sefirot* there is no judgment, only mercy." (The *Sefirot* are represented in the Kabbalah's "Tree of Life" as the 10 attributes of God. It is of interest to note that the Godly attributes Justice and Mercy are associated with the colors red and white, and the quality of Beauty, balances them. Does this make you think of "Beautiful Savior?" And I cannot help but think of our Savior on the cross holding His arms out for us all the day long, balancing justice and mercy on Eternal Scales that only He could implement.)

There is yet another astounding "red to white" reference found in Yoma 39b of the Talmud:

> Our Rabbis taught: During the last forty years before the destruction of the Temple [Titus destroyed the Temple in 70 A.D. Who died during this crucial time?] the lot ('For the Lord') did not come up in the right hand: nor did the crimson-coloured strap become white . . . and the doors of the *Hekal* [Temple] would open by themselves, until R. Johanan b. Zakkai rebuked them, saying: "Hekal, Hekal, why wilt thou be the alarmer thyself? I know about thee that thou wilt be destroyed, for Zechariah ben Ido has already prophesied concerning thee: Open thy doors, O Lebanon, that the fire may devour thy cedars.
>
> R. Isaac b. Tablai said: Why is its name called Lebanon? Because it makes white the sins of Israel. (Emphasis added.)

According to this Jewish legend, the scarlet wool tied to the door of the Temple during the Day of Atonement ritual, ceased to miraculously turn white in the approximate year of 30 A.D. What incredible event occurred at about this time that superceded yearly sacrifices for the atoning of Israel and, indeed, all mankind? The great and once-and-for-all Sacrifice of Jesus Christ.

And why did Rabbi Yohanan ben Zakkai connect the verse in Zechariah to the destruction of the Temple? We need to view these verses by looking for another layer of encoded meaning, a "Bible Code" if you will, the code of symbolism. In First Kings chapter 5 in verses 8 and 10, the agreements between King Solomon and Hiram of Tyre, the kingly building supplier from Lebanon, are discussed. The following words lay an important groundwork:

> And Hiram sent to Solomon, saying, I have considered the things which thou sentest to me for: and I will do all thy desire concerning timber of **cedar** and timber of **fir**.
>
> So Hiram gave Solomon **cedar** trees and **fir** trees according to all his desire." (Emphasis added.)

Now let's look at the verses Rabbi Johanan believed were predicting the destruction of the Temple by the Romans:

> Open thy doors, O Lebanon, that the fire may devour thy cedars.
>
> Howl, fir tree; for the cedar is fallen; because the mighty are spoiled: howl, O ye oaks of Bashan; for the forest of the vintage is come down. Zech. 11:1-2.

Could "cedar" and "fir" be cues to point us to the Temple? And could the rabbis be correct making the connection between Lebanon and the Temple? It might help to know that Lebanon comes from a root word that means "to whiten."

There is another instance where Lebanon is interpreted to mean the temple. This is also found in the Talmud and concerns Rabbi Jochanan Ben Zaccai who was carried out of Jerusalem hidden in a coffin, during the first Roman siege of the Holy City. He asked to be taken to the general Vespasian who was then leading the Roman forces, and after admittance, addressed Vespasian with "Live, O king, live, O king." The Talmud records: "Saith Vespasian, You salute me as if I were king, but I am not so; and the king will hear this, and judge such a one to death. To whom he [Jochanan, said], Although you are not king yet, you shall be so, *for this temple must not be destroyed but by a king's hand*, as it is written, 'Lebanon shall fall by a mighty one,' " Isaiah 10:34[16] (emphasis in the original).

By A.D. 69, Vespasian was made emperor and his son, Titus, resumed the campaign against the Jews. In 70 A.D. Titus conquered Jerusalem and destroyed the Temple. He also followed his father to the emperor's throne. The Temple indeed fell to "kings."

I just have to mention another marvelous red-to-white reference that taught me a whole new way of understanding the principle of fasting. *The Zohar* quotes Rabbi Abba who said:

> Sin is red, as it says, 'Though your sins be as scarlet;' man puts the sacrificial animal on fire, which is also red; the priest sprinkles the red blood round the altar, but the smoke ascending to heaven is white. Thus the red is turned to white: the attribute of Justice is turned into the attribute of Mercy. . . R. Isaac said: Red (blood) and white (fat) are offered for sacrifice, and odour ascends from both. The spices of incense are in part red and in part white—frankincense is white, pure myrrh is red—and the odour ascends from red and white. Moreover, it is written, 'To offer unto me the fat and the blood' (Ezekiel 34:15)— again white and red. Hence as a substitute for this (since

the destruction of the temple) man sacrifices his own fat and blood (by fasting) and so obtains atonement. As the lily, which is red and white, is turned entirely into white by means of fire, so the sacrificial animal is turned entirely into white (smoke) by means of fire. Also at the present time (when there are no sacrifices) when a man offers in his fast his fat and his blood, the sacrifice has to go through fire if it is to be turned into white (bring down mercy), for, said R. Judah, fasting weakens the limbs and causes the body to burn, and just then is the appropriate time to offer up the fat and the blood on that fire; and it is this which is called 'an altar of atonement.'[17]

Sacrifices were meant to forever turn us to our God, to draw us to Him, to thank Him for His loving kindness and forgiveness. Sacrifices pointed the way for a special substitute for the yearly atonement of sin—for the Once-And-For-All-Time Sacrifice of the Savior.

The yearly "Sacrifice of Sacrifices," the rite of Yom Kippur, (Day of Atonement), was truly fulfilled once and forever when the pure white, spotless Lamb of God came to take away the sins of the world. As white signifies mercy, the scarlet robes of Christ at his Second Coming will signify judgment upon those who have and will yet scorn this great gift of Jesus Christ.

There's a wonderful old hymn called "Jesus Paid It All." My favorite lyrics are: "Sin had left a crimson stain—He washed it white as snow."

Red to white! Making our garments white in the blood of the Lamb—this is the great mystery taught to those who have come to know and love the Man of Galilee, the Son of God, the Red Heifer of Mercy and Justice, Jesus the Christ.

Red and White in the Land of Israel: The First Will Be Last

The hardest part of writing this book has been to realize that I have far more research material than I can use. But I feel that Joel's wine and milk reference must also be included. Remember when Christ said in Matthew 19:30: "But many that are first shall be last; and the last shall be first." I believe that Joel has a special prophecy about that glorious day when those who first heard Him preach, the sons and daughters of Judah, will at last come to know Jesus Christ. In Joel 3:18-21 it reads:

> And it shall come to pass in that day, that the mountains shall drop down new wine, and the hills shall flow with milk, and all the rivers of Judah shall flow with waters, and a fountain shall come forth of the house of the Lord, and shall water the valley of Shittim.
>
> Egypt shall be a desolation, and Edom shall be a desolate wilderness, for the violence against the children of Judah, because they have shed innocent blood in their land.
>
> But Judah shall dwell for ever, and Jerusalem from generation to generation.
>
> For I will cleanse their blood that I have not cleansed: for the Lord dwelleth in Zion.

I see that sequence of scriptures as foretelling "that day" when the first will be the last to come to the Holy One of Israel—to see the wounds in His hands and feet and to accept Him as Messiah. At that time, a national cleansing and regeneration will take place. Truly a fountain will be opened up for Israel. Ezekiel 36:25 explains that the Lord says He will "sprinkle clean water upon you, and ye shall be clean: from all your filthiness, and from all your idols, will I cleanse you."

This verse is read as a "*haftorah*" along with Numbers 19 during the weekly Torah portion as the Jews identify the "clean water" as the Water of Purification or the water with Ashes of the Red Heifer. The Lord has not forgotten His people Israel. They will blessed at His hand. They will be given the miracle that turns red to white.

Finding More Examples

While the three "Day of Atonement" red and white references above and Joel's prophecy are the most pertinent to this study, I cannot resist sharing a few more examples with you from Jewish sources.

In the beginning of Rabbi Adin Steinsaltz's *The Thirteen Petalled Rose* he quotes the *Zohar's* commentary on Song of Songs 2:2:

> What is the rose—Knesset Yisrael, the Community of Israel. For there is a rose (above) and a rose (below). Just as the rose which is among the thorns has red and white, so does Knesset Yisrael have justice and mercy. Just as a rose has thirteen petals, so does Knesset Yisrael have thirteen measures of compassion encompassing it on all sides.
>
> . . . Five strong petals surround the rose, and these five, called salvations, are five gates. Concerning which secret it is written: 'I will lift up the cup of salvation . . .' (Psalms 116:13) (Emphasis added.)

In E.W. Bullinger's *Number in Scripture,* he explains some of the reasons why he believes five is the number of grace. He writes that "if four is the number of the world, then it represents man's weakness, and helplessness and vanity . . . But four plus one (4 + 1 = 5) is significant of Divine strength added to and made perfect in that weakness; of omnipotence combined with the impotence of earth; of Divine favour uninfluenced and invincible." Bullinger then mentions that favor "shown to the unworthy is called GRACE!" In telling how the Lord changed Abram's name to signify the covenant which had been made, Bullinger says the Lord dropped the Hebrew letter "*hey* or h," one of the letters of His own name, YHWH, into Abram's name:

> [W]hen God changed Abram's name to Abraham (Gen.
> 17:5), the change was made very simply, but very
> significantly (for there is no chance with God), by
> inserting in the middle of it the fifth letter of the alphabet,
> (the Hebrew Hey), the symbol of the number five . . . All
> this was of grace and it is stamped with this significance."[18]

So we find that a wise Jewish teacher connects the Cup of Salvation
with the number five—in which the learned Christian scholar Bullinger
sees grace.

Steinsaltz expounds on this idea as he explains the ceremonies in each
Jewish home on the eve of the Sabbath, where ". . . the dwelling is made
into a sanctuary. The table on which are set the white loaves [the braided
challah] and the burning candles recall the Holy Temple with its menorah
and its shew bread. The table itself is, as always, a reminder of the altar in
the Temple . . ."

Steinsaltz discusses the Kiddush cup and the wine that is partaken of
during this ceremony.

> Red wine especially expresses a certain aspect of the
> Sefirah of Gevurah, which also has an aspect of severity
> and justice. Thus after one has poured most of the wine
> into the cup, a little water, symbol of grace and love, is
> added to create the right mixture, or harmony, between
> Hesed [Mercy] and Gevurah [Justice]. After the filling of
> the cup . . .one places it on the palm of the right hand in
> such a way that the cup, supported by the upturned
> fingers, resembles or recalls a rose. (Emphasis added.)[19]

Another "coincidence" is to be found in the account of when the
Savior's side was pierced with the Roman sword and a mixture of blood and
water poured out. "The right mixture" and "harmony"? *The Encyclopedia*

Talmudica states that "Blood mixed with water, if the mixture is red, counts as blood for . . . sacrificial sprinkling on the altar."[20] Father Leopold Sabourin adds another intriguing insight when he quotes the Targum of Pseudo Jonathan (Jerusalem I) about Exodus 17:7 where Moses struck the rock and water flowed: "Moses struck the rock twice; the first time blood flowed and the second, water."[21] Certainly Christians can see the sweetness of "grace" in that moment when symbolism became reality. What the Savior "poured out" in His death on the cross brings life to us all.

The Daughter of Seven

One last very complicated example of the red-to-white metaphor is also found in the Zohar. If you will be patient and wade through this with me, I believe you will find some "hidden treasures" that have to do with the Red Heifer, the numbers five and seven and covenants!

I will quote the translation made by Aryeh Wineman[22] because of the clarity of his language. The tale is of an unfortunate man (named Eliazer, *El azar*, "God has helped," or "God is my helper" which is, again 'coincidentally,' the name of the priest who sacrificed the first Red Heifer) who, while traveling with his sister, partook of too much wine and found himself in an intimate embrace that came close to incest. Later, through his trying to quell a brawl at the inn where he and his sister were staying, he was badly injured. He was healed by a rabbi, though he retained a mark on his face.

Eliazer was questioned by another rabbi as to this mark on his face so he said, " . . . from that very day I have engaged in repentance. Each day I see my face in a mirror and I cry before the Holy One, blessed be He, Master of the worlds, concerning that sin, and with those tears I wash my face." The rabbi suggested that Eliazer repeat a verse from Isaiah three times ("Your guilt shall depart and your sins be purged away") and the mark vanished.

Upon a later meeting of these two men, when Eliazer found out that this was the rabbi who had told him how to lose the mark of his sin, he invited the rabbi to his home where he prepared "three measures of bread and the meat of a three-year-old calf."[23] Eliazer told the rabbi that the mother of the calf whose meat had supplied the meal had been a red heifer and there was a strange experience about this red heifer that puzzled him. Wineman's translation is as follows: ". . . one day, quite some time before she calved, as I was leading her to pasture to graze, a man passed before me and inquired of me as to the heifer's name. I told him I had never given her a name. The man declared, 'She will be called Bat-sheva, the mother of Solomon—should you merit atonement.' And when I turned around to see the man, he was gone."

The rabbi explained, "Certainly it is a mystery alluding to both the upper and lower worlds. In esoteric teaching a certain sefirah is actually called *Bat-sheva* (the daughter of seven) [and is referred to as a red heifer]. And therefore all things (in Numbers 19) occur in groups of seven : seven cows, seven burnings, seven sprinklings, seven washings, seven times the term tame (impure, unclean), seven times the term tahor (clean, pure) and seven priests—including Moses and Aaron who are mentioned by name in this passage. It is correct, as that man said who designated the name Bat-sheva, that it is entirely a mystery."

Wineman explains in his notes at the end of this chapter that the *sefirah* referred to is the *Shekinah* (Malkut, being the lowest of the seven lower *Sefirot*, hence derives from all those above). The *Shekinah*, described as the 'perfect red one' in terms of Her compassionate type of judgment, is symbolized by the Red Heifer."[24]

I believe that followers of Jesus Christ might be able to solve the mystery associated with Batsheba. I spent a number of long nights with a pile of reference books (providing knowledge) and a lot of pondering (providing faith) before I thought of the following connections. And I place these conjectures here knowing that minds more faithful and learned than mine may be able to come up with a more enlightened explanation.

Many old reference works that I trust were written before "critical thinking" and "The Jesus Seminar" started to pick apart the Word of God using a lot of worldly and scholarly pride. In several of these old biblical encyclopedias I found that "Batsheva/Batsheba" means "daughter of seven" which is certainly logical because "*bat*" means daughter and "*sheva*" is seven. (Know that the letters "b" and "v" are interchangeable which is why you will see both "Abraham" and "Avraham" in Jewish writings.)

But Batsheba is also translated "daughter of the oath." This puzzled me until I confirmed it by checking concordances where I found that the word "oath," *shebuah,* comes from the root word for seven. A little more digging turned up the fact that Beer-Sheba was named for the covenant made between Abraham and Abimelech noted in Gen. 21:32. Chapter 21 tells about Hagar being sent into the wilderness with her son Ishmael and then comes the tale of the covenant. (And I found it interesting that the word used is not "oath" but "covenant.") So Batsheba can rightly be called "Daughter of the Covenant."

There is good reason why Abraham would connect the number seven with covenants and oaths and it is more than the fact that there were seven wells at Beer-Sheba.. You have only to read Psalm 12:6—"The words of the Lord are pure words: as silver tried in a furnace of earth, purified seven times"—to understand the significance of the number seven in scripture. In fact, that very verse in Psalms, was interpreted by R. Hanan b. Pazzi in the Midrash Rabbah (Numbers Vol. II, page 748) "as applying to the Biblical section dealing with the Red Heifer, which contains seven mentions of seven things."

When we look at the number of times you find "seven" in the Book of Revelation, we can't help but realize that it is a sacred number. But it was significant in Jewish thought as well. In the Dead Sea Scroll fragment 4Q403 I, i, 1-29, a fragment found at Masada, is the following psalm. In the original there are many brackets which indicate missing letters that have been supplied by the translator. I have eliminated the brackets and emphasized the word "seven."

Psalm of singing uttered by the tongue of the seventh of the sovereign Princes, a powerful song to the God of holiness with its seven marvellous songs. He shall sing to the King of holiness seven times with seven words of wonderful songs; seven psalms singing his blessings; seven psalms of magnification of his righteousness; seven psalms of exaltation of his kingship; seven psalms of praises of his glory; seven psalms of thanksgiving for his marvellous deeds; seven psalms of exultation of his power; seven psalms singing his holiness; . . . seven times with wonderful words, words of . . ."[25] (There are even seven attributes of the Lord mentioned here: his blessings, his righteousness, his kingship, his glory, his marvelous deeds, his power and his holiness!)

In Deut. 28:3-8 the Lord gives an incredible pattern of sevens for those who keep His commandments:

Blessed shall thou be in the city, and blessed thou shalt be in the field. Blessed shall be the fruit of thy body, and the fruit of thy ground, and the fruit of thy cattle, the increase of thy kine, and the flocks of thy sheep. Blessed shall be thy basket and thy store. Blessed shalt thou be when thou comest in, and blessed shalt thou be when thou goest out. The Lord shall cause thine enemies that rise up against thee to be smitten before thy face: they shall come out against thee one way, and flee before thee seven ways. The Lord shall command the blessing upon thee in thy storehouses, and in all that thou settest thine hand unto; and he shall bless thee in the land which the Lord thy God giveth thee.

This exact pattern is repeated in the negative for those who keep not the Lord's commandments in verses 15-20 and 25:

> Cursed thou shalt be in the city, and cursed thou shalt be in the field. Cursed shall be thy basket and thy store. Cursed shall be the fruit of thy body, and the fruit of thy land, the increase of thy kine, and the flocks of thy sheep. Cursed shalt thou be when thou comest in, and cursed shalt thou be when thou goest out. The Lord shall send upon thee cursing, vexation, and rebuke, in all that thou settest thine hand unto for to do, until thou be destroyed, and until thou perish quickly; because of the wickedness of thy doings, whereby thou hast forsaken me. . . The Lord shall cause thee to be smitten before thine enemies: thou shalt go out but one way against them, and flee seven ways before them: and shalt be removed into all the kingdoms of the earth.

Can you see the pattern here?
Blessed Cursed
Blessed Cursed
Blessed Cursed
Blessed Cursed
Blessed Cursed
Blessed Cursed
Seven Cursing
Blessing Seven

In Genesis chapter 28 I found the number seven repeated seven times. Three times in English as seven and four times as "Beer-sheba" where *sheba* means seven. That fact alone is a clue to know that there is more going on here than the simple story, if you understand Bullinger's theories from *Number in Scripture.*

After Abraham and Abimelech discuss an oath not to deal falsely, Abraham brings up a problem where the servants of Abimelech had violently taken away a well of water that belonged to Abraham. For the oath about not dealing falsely, Abraham gave sheep and oxen to Abimelech (verse 27) and the men made a covenant. Verses 28-31 say: "And Abraham set seven ewe lambs of the flock by themselves. And Abimelech said unto Abraham, What mean these seven ewe lambs, which thou hast set by themselves? And he said, For these seven ewe lambs shalt thou take of my hand that they may be a witness unto me, that I have digged this well. Wherefore he called that place Beer-Sheba; because there they sware both of them."

In a commentary on Genesis by S.R. Driver, D.D., he writes:

> The stress laid on the number 'seven' in vv. 28-30 seems to shew that the writer intends to explain 'Beer-sheba' as meaning 'Well of seven' . . . but in v. 31 it is explained expressly as meaning 'Well of swearing.'[26]

Driver further suggests that these words may mean 'to seven-oneself' or to pledge oneself in some way by seven sacred things. He also says in a footnote that Herodotus writes that the Arabs, when a solemn oath is being concluded, smear seven stones with blood drawn from the hands of the contracting parties.

Dummelow's commentary also concurs that:

> The place was henceforth called Beer-sheba "well of the seven" or "well of the oath," because the covenant had been ratified by the sacred or perfect number seven which was the usual number of things sworn by.[27]

Oaths and covenants lead us back to what God promises us. He initiated covenants with Israel to provide a yearly way of dealing with sin.

Christ came to "fill full" all those covenants that were but types and shadows of the "New Covenant" where the blood of Christ became the New Testament. (1Cor. 11:25.)

So we have the seven things mentioned seven times in Numbers 19, the chapter about the Red Heifer. There is a story in the *Zohar* where a man is purged from his sin and has a Red Heifer that is mysteriously named "Batsheba" or daughter of seven or daughter of the oath. We read about "five strong petals" of the rose that were also called "gates." We learned from Bullinger that five is the number of grace. And we found a chapter in Genesis where seven is mentioned seven times in connection with oaths and covenants. And we definitely know that Batshebah and the Red Heifer are "mysterious!"

Let's see how God has quietly honored some of His daughters. So take a quick jump to Matthew's genealogy of Christ in chapter one. There are around forty men who are listed but only five women: **Tamar**, who bore Judah's twin sons, and who seems to tell us through her life story that sometimes to obtain the blessings promised you, subterfuge must be employed. (And Jacob was a great example of this, with Esau and Laban.) **Rahab** (yes, the prostitute of Jericho), who is living proof that when you repent, your sins are washed away forever. Washed clean enough to merit being an ancestress of the Messiah! **Ruth**, whose sweet story notes that you don't have to have to be born into the "correct" lineage or race to receive God's gifts. You can even be a "gentile" or a foreigner. *Her That Had Been The Wife Of Urias*, a very strange, "mysterious" or cloaked way of saying Batsheba, a woman who was probably taken against her will (I believe she was raped—in the biblical culture, how would you tell the powerful King David "no"??) and became pregnant because of it. Batsheba, the woman whom Nathan the prophet called "one little ewe lamb" and "was unto him like a daughter [Hebrew: *bat*]" (2 Samuel 12:3). And finally, **Mary**, the obedient young virgin of Nazareth.

I'd like to linger on the name Mary, which in Hebrew is Miriam. After checking a number of sources, I found only questions marks, literally. One source said, "seeress or lady?" and yet others suggested "rebellion." When you think of the first well-known "Miriam," perhaps a glimmer of understanding comes.

Moses's sister Miriam, was much loved by the Israelites. Yet she rebelled against Moses and was stricken with leprosy. Moses prayed for her and she was healed. Could the term "rebellion" associated with Miriam also take us back to the original rebellion: the sin in the Garden of Eden and the ongoing battle between the serpent and the "seed of the woman"? (Genesis 3: 15.) Was not the woman the first to "rebel" against God's commandment not to partake of the fruit of the Tree of Knowledge of Good and Evil?

When you read this verse in Genesis: "And I will put enmity between thee and the woman, and between thy seed and her seed; it shall bruise thy head, and thou shalt bruise his heel," do you realize that there is only one instance of the Seed of the Woman? You and I are descended from the seed of the man and the woman, but only Jesus Christ is Seed of the Woman!

I love what Charles Spurgeon wrote about this particular Messianic prophecy:

> It was a thing unheard of before, and unparalleled since, that a virgin should conceive and bear a Son. The first promise ran thus, 'The seed of the woman,' not the offspring of the man. Since venturous woman led the way into the sin which brought forth Paradise lost, she, and she alone, ushers in the Regainer of Paradise.[28]

Is there not an element of grace involved in the role of Woman in bringing forth the Regainer of Paradise? When you think of the symbolism God wants us to understand in the Sacrifice of the Red Heifer, is it possible that in mandating a first-born female (heifer) rather than a first-born male (or bull), God is pointing us to grace and mercy?

I will close this discussion of the meaning of "Miriam" or Mary, with a quotation from one of my all-time favorite books, *Ancient Secrets*, by Rabbi Levi Meier:

> Miriam had also been beloved by the people. Her name, tradition has it, meant 'one who turns bitter water sweet,' and the Israelites believed that it was because of her that they had always had miraculous access to drinking water. (Emphasis added.)[29]

What a perfect "type" Moses' sister Miriam was! Yet another Miriam, in a stable in Bethlehem, would be the means by which the true source of "Living Water" would come forth to Israel and all the world—to forever change the bitter to sweet through His atoning sacrifice.

Could the "five strong petals" be the "gates of grace" or the women through which the Merciful Christ came into the world to offer Himself as a sinless sacrifice for sin? Do these mysteries point to the Seed of the Woman, to Jeremiah's "for the Lord hath created a new thing in the earth, A woman shall compass a man" (Jer. 31:22)? Where a mortal woman bore the Son of God? Could a female red calf point to the grace and mercy of Christ washing away our sins?

Red to white, sevens, fives and Red Heifers. Clues to understanding the great mystery of Redemption.

1. *A New Standard Bible Dictionary,* Funk & Wagnalls Company, 1926, page 938.
2. *Menachoth, 8, 6, Mishayoth, Vol. 5, Order Kodashim,* Judaica Press, Ltd. Gateshead, England, 1983, page 141.
3. Eliyahu Kitav, *The Book of Our Heritage, II Adar-Nisan,* Feldheim Publishers, Jerusalem, New York, Revised Edition, 1978, page 106.
4. *The Zohar,* translated by Harry Sperling, Maurice Simon, The Soncino Press, London, New York, 1984, Vol. II, page 360.
5. Matthew Henry, *Commentary on the Whole Bible,* Hendrickson Publishers, 1991, page 1187.
6. Adam Clarke, *Commentary on the Old Testament,* Vol. 4, G. Lane & P.P. Sandford, 1843, page 211.
7. Alfred Edersheim, D.D., Ph.D., *Sketches of Jewish Social Life in the Days of Christ,* Wm. B. Eerdmans Publishing Company, 1982, page 293.
8. David H. Stern, *The Jewish New Testament,* Jewish New Testament Publications, Jerusalem, 1988, page 62.
9. *Guide to the Treasures of the Temple Exhibit,* The Temple Institute, n.d., Jerusalem, page 9.
10. Rabbi Adin Steinsaltz, *The Talmud: Steinsaltz Edition, A Reference Guide,* Random House, New York, 1989, page 209.
11. *Midrash Rabbah,* Vol. 7, Deuteronomy, Lamentations, translated by Rev. J. Rabbinowitz, B.A., Ph.D., The Soncino Press, 1983, page 1.
12. Jacob Neusner has an informative section in *First Century Judaism in Crisis,* regarding Boethus. On pages 72-73 he writes: "A popular song preserved in Pharisaic literature went:

   > *Woe unto me, because of the house of Boethus*
   > *Woe unto me because of their clubs!*
   > *Woe unto me because of the house of Hanin*
   > *Woe unto me because of their whisperings!*
   > *Woe unto me because of the house of Kathros,*
   > *Woe unto me because of their quills.*
   > *Woe unto me because of the house of Ishmael ben Phiabi,*
   > *Woe unto me because of their fists.*
   >
   > *For they are high priests,*
   > *And their sons are treasurers,*
   > *And their sons-in-law are law-officers,*
   > *And their slaves beat the folks with sticks.*

   Neusner also quotes Josephus who reported: "Hananiah likewise had servants who were very wicked. They joined themselves to the boldest sort of people, and went to the threshing floors and took away by violence the tithes that belonged to the priests. They did not refrain from beating those who would not give these tithes to them. So the other high priests acted in like manner, as did his servants. No one was able to stop them, so that some of the priests who were accustomed to being supported from those tithes died for want of food." These examples of priestly corruption make the Essene's withdrawal to Qumran more understandable and confirm the words of Christ who said: "Ye have made my house a den of thieves."

13. Judah Nadich, *Legends of the Rabbis: Vol. I, Jewish Legends of the Second Commonwealth,* Jason Aronson, Inc., 1994, page 110.

14. Rabbi Yitzchak Abarbanel, *The Abarbanel on the Yom Kippur Service in the Beis HaMikdash,* Targum/Feldham, Israel, 1990, page 31.

15. Louis Jacobs, ed., *The Schocken Book of Jewish Mystical Testimonies,* Schocken Books, New York, 1977, page 105.

16. *Gittin,* fol.56, I. et Echah Rabbathi, fol. 64.2, quoted in *A Commentary on the New Testament from the Talmud and Hebraica: Matthew -1 Corinthians,* Vol. 1, Place Names in the Gospels, John Lightfoot, Hendrickson Publishers, 1989, page 375.

17. *The Zohar,* translated by Harry Sperling, Maurice Simon, The Soncino Press, London, New York, 1984, Vol. III, pages 66-67.

18. E.W. Bullinger, *Number in Scripture,* Kregel Publications, 1967, pages 135-136.

19. Rabbi Adin Steinsaltz, *The Thirteen Petalled Rose,* Jason Aronson Inc., 1992, 1980, pages 176-179.

20. *Encyclopedia Talmudica,* Vol. I, Israel, 1969, page 201.

21. Leopold Sabourin, S.J., *The Names and Titles of Jesus,* The Macmillan Company, 1967, page 122.

22. Aryah Wineman, *Mystic Tales from the Zohar,* Jewish Publication Society, 1997, pages 127-128.

23. It is of interest that this is the same meal that Abraham served to his heavenly visitors in Genesis 18:6-7 where the three holy men receive "three measures of fine meal" and "a calf tender and good."

24. Aryah Wineman, op cited, page 131.

25. Geza Vermes, *The Dead Sea Scrolls in English,* Revised and Extended Fourth Edition, Penguin Books, London, 1995, page 257.

26. S.R. Driver, *The Book of Genesis,* Methuen & Co., London, Fifth Edition, 1906, page 215.

27. *A Commentary on the Whole Bible,* edited by J.R. Dummelow, Macmillan and Company, Limited, London, 1919, page 29.

28. Charles Haddon Spurgeon, *Morning and Evening Daily Readings,* Zondervan, 1977, page 720.

29. Rabbi Levi Meier, *Ancient Secrets: Using the Stories of the Bible to Improve Our Everyday Lives,* Villard Books, 1996, page 219.

Chapter Seven

The Messiah of the Winepress

Came at length the dreadful night;
Vengeance with its iron rod
Stood, and with collected might
Bruised the harmless Lamb of God.
See, my soul, thy Savior see,
Prostrate in Gethsemane!
Charles Haddon Spurgeon [1]

What terrors did that dark night in a garden on the Mount of Olives hold for the Holy One of Israel? In Gethsemane as He first knelt and then lay prostrate beneath the weight of some appalling grief—what exactly was the cup He asked to have bypass Him? For something so dreaded, so unimaginably horrible occurred while His disciples slept that as Spurgeon continues, "From His blessed person there distilled a bloody sweat, for His soul was exceedingly sorrowful even unto death."

Dummelow's commentary suggests that: "Great mental agony has been known to produce this phenomenon" [2] of great drops of blood as it were sweat. Was Christ asking that the horrors of crucifixion be taken away from Him? Was He afraid to die on the cross? I agree with what Adam

159

Clarke said about this: "it is fully evident that the *fear of death* could have had no place in the mind of our blessed Lord. He was in the bloom of life, in perfect health, and had never suffered any thing from disease of any kind; this sweat was most assuredly produced by a preternatural cause."[3]

And on page 447 of *The Life of Christ*, Farrar writes:

> The Christian hardly needs to be told that it was no such vulgar fear [of death] which forced from his Saviour that sweat of blood. No, it was something infinitely more than this: infinitely more than the highest stretch of our imagination can realize.

We may not have spent much time pondering Christ's time in the Garden of Gethsemane and just what caused Him to bleed from every pore. Our attention seems to have been focused on the horrors of crucifixion.

It is difficult for us to understand the blessed condescension of the Creator of this earth *allowing* Himself to be crucified. Yes, we know that literally thousands of men met their deaths on a Roman cross as did our Savior. But here is the truly unthinkable: the Son of God *allowed* and *willingly* went to His death by crucifixion.

Victims of crucifixion often lingered in agony for days before death ended their suffering. But we must remember that Christ suffered from three bloody tortures: the agony in the Garden of Gethsemane, the scourging (the bits of metal and bone on the ends of the multi-strap whip used, literally flayed the skin on the back to the bone; men often died from being scourged) and the Cross. (E.W. Bullinger notes that "the number three is associated with the Godhead, for there are 'three persons in one God.' "[4])

If we think for a moment about the excruciating pains Christ suffered in His scourging ("The plowers plowed upon my back: they made long their furrows." Psalms 129:3) and in those six hours on the cross, it's almost impossible for us to comprehend what greater agony could have caused Him to sweat blood in Gethsemane. Surely it was not fear. There had to have been some other unique suffering in that garden that only Christ could have endured.

Henry W. Soltau (1805-1875) made this insightful comment:

> Believers are often too apt to dwell exclusively on the bodily sufferings of our blessed Lord on the cross, instead of contemplating, as far as we are permitted to do, the unspeakable sorrows of Jesus in His soul under the stripes of God, "when it pleased Jehovah to bruise Him; when His soul was made an offering for sin, and he poured his soul unto death.[5]

Isaiah's haunting "Suffering Servant" chapter tells us:

> But he was wounded for our transgressions, he was bruised for our iniquities: the chastisement of our peace was upon him; and with his stripes we are healed. . . Yet it pleased the Lord to bruise him. (53:4-5, 10)

We will come back to this word "bruised" shortly. Spurgeon cautions us with this remark: "The outward sorrows of crucifixion ye know, but the inward griefs ye do not know, for what our Lord endured was beyond what any mortal man could have borne."[6]

The German theologian F.W. Krummacher (1796-1868) wrote a magnificent book called *The Suffering Savior: Meditations on the Last Days of Christ* (Kregel Publications, 1992). Krummacher wrote of three causes of Christ's agony in the Garden of Gethsemane. First: "his horror of sin, by amazement at the abominations of our misdeeds. . . Only imagine personified holiness placed in the midst of the pool of the world's corruption!"

Second: Christ experienced the curse of sin—in "being separated from God, deprived of His favor, estranged from His affection."

And perhaps the most chilling, "The third cause of our Lord's bitter distress in Gethsemane is to be sought in the world of fallen spirits. It is beyond a doubt that Satan essentially contributed to the horrors of that scene. The Lord Himself intimates as much in the words, 'The prince of this world cometh,' and 'This is the hour and the power of darkness'. . . Here the complaints of Psalm 18 were realized: 'The sorrows of death compassed me, and the floods of ungodly men men made me afraid. The sorrows of hell compassed me about, the snares of death prevented me.'" (Pages 108-112.)

To the testimony of the above writers, I add my conviction that we must understand that lonesome struggle. We must know that something incredibly holy and tender happened in that garden on the Mount of Olives and it had to do with Christ's atoning sacrifice for us all. And again, the Red Heifer, slain on that same mount, can be a symbolic type and shadow to teach us of our Lord's sweet work of redemption.

Keep in mind that only the totally Red Heifer was slain on the Mount of Olives. Also, the heifer of Numbers 19 was the only sacrificial animal that had to be of a certain color by commandment from the Lord.

The mysterious Red Heifer ritual points symbolically to something extremely significant that occurred among those hillside olive groves. And I believe there are three insight-laden scriptures about Christ treading the winepress alone (Genesis 49:11, Isaiah 63:1-3, Revelation 19:13) that will explain a connection between the Red Heifer, Christ's blood-stained robe in the Garden of Gethsemane and His red raiment at His Second Coming.

And as I pondered and prayed to understand the connection between the Red Heifer on the Mount of Olives and the Lord Jesus Christ, I was led to scriptural witnesses and to the writings of a number of godly men who testify to the Divinity of the Savior. I believe that the worth of this chapter for the reader is in the collection of these writings that I share with you now.

Why Talk About *Winepresses* on the Mount of *Olives*?

When you walk up the gently sloping Mount of Olives, you see OLIVE TREES. The very word Gethsemane, is *Gat-Shemanim* in Hebrew, which very-literally translated means "the winepress of oil" or "oil press." Those who have been to Israel have vivid memories of the massive stone olive presses at Capernaum. Why the emphasis on winepresses in this chapter?

The very first time I stepped on the Mount of Olives, I was shown, of course, the twisted and gnarled olive trees that still stand after nearly two millennia at the traditional site of the Garden of

An ancient olive tree in the Garden of Gethsemane

Gethsemane. It is known that Titus cut down every tree surrounding Jerusalem during his siege and even salted the earth to show his complete victory over the Jews. The ancient olive trees in the garden at the Church of All Nations (the traditional site of the Garden of Gethsemane) may be shoots that sprang up from the decimated trees of Christ's day.

An Olive Press at Capernaum

Botanists Harold N. and Alma L. Moldenke note that anciently "gardens" were often a miscellany of trees jumbled together, more like thickets rather than gardens. They write: "Gethsemane was such an olive orchard 'garden' at the foot of the Mount of Olives, where the oil-presses were located."[7]

But I was also shown an ancient winepress on those slopes. (I do have a photo of the winepress, but since there are so many winepresses throughout Israel, I could not find a written description of this particular winepress.) You do not press olives the same way you press grapes. There is no mistaking a winepress for an olive press!

My tour guide made an off-handed mention that since it takes at least 10 years for olive trees to begin to bear once they are planted, often grape vines are planted among them.

I found this statement verified in a well-researched book called *Encyclopedia of Bible Life* by Madeleine S. and J. Lane Miller (Harper & Brothers, 1944). On page 410 the Millers write:

> On still another occasion, Jesus set the scene of one of his famous stories in a vineyard. He used the well-known fact that **often fruit trees were grown among vines**—especially fig, and **often olive** and mulberry trees. This was allowed by Mosaic laws, which forbade planting more than one variety of grapes in a vineyard. It also enabled a man literally to 'sit under his own vine and fig tree;' for while vines were usually allowed to trail along the ground, with only stout sticks to prop them up, when bearing clusters, they were often trained onto trees or over trellises. (Emphasis added.)

I have read a beautiful explanation of Christ's suffering in Gethsemane where the author tried to make the "press" scriptures fit an olive press. As you read on, I hope you will see that a winepress makes much more sense biblically.

The Mount of Olives and the Winepress in Prophecy

I find it intriguing that Jesus Christ would appear twice in the world's history on the Mount of Olives in red robes. The first time was in the Garden of Gethsemane where His bloody sweat surely stained His garments. Spurgeon notes this in two places:

> He went down into Gethsemane, and there He prayed earnestly; but with sweet submission; for He said, "Nevertheless, not as I will, but as thou wilt." Complete submission was the essential spirit of His prayer. He rose up from prayer <u>all crimson with his bloody sweat</u>, and He went to meet His foes, delivering Himself up voluntarily to be led as a sheep to the slaughter.[8] (Emphasis added.)

And also:

> He went forth to fight with all the adversaries of our souls, even with all the powers of darkness. It was a terrible battle. How thick and fast the shafts flew at the commencement of the fight! Our hero soon knew the garments rolled in blood, for <u>He became covered with a bloody sweat</u>.[9] (Emphasis added.)

We are told that Christ will be arrayed in red raiment at the judgment of the Second Coming. Zechariah 14:4 specifically tells us where He will come:

> And his feet shall stand in that day upon the Mount of Olives, which is before Jerusalem on the east, and the mount of Olives shall cleave in the midst thereof toward the east and toward the west, and there shall be a great valley; and half of the mountain shall remove toward the north, and half of it toward the south.

We find documentation about the Messiah and His red raiment in three scriptures ("in the mouth of two or three witnesses every word may be established" Matthew 18:16):

(1.) <u>The first verse</u> about clothing stained red from wine is found in Genesis 49:11:

> Binding his foal unto the vine, and his ass's colt unto the choice vine; **he washed his garments in wine, and his clothes in the blood of grapes**." (emphasis added).

The Zohar notes that this verse has hidden references to the Holy Name "*Yah*" which is the shortened version of the name *Yahweh, Yahveh* or Jehovah. If you have a copy of *The Jerusalem Bible*, printed in Israel by Koren Publishing, you can find these clues in the Hebrew text. In this edition or in scrolls written by Orthodox Torah scholars, you will find anomalies such as Hebrew letters written larger than the regular text or written smaller. Some letters are upside down. Sometimes extra or superfluous letters are added to words. These different-sized and extra letters are thought to be clues to hidden meanings.

In this story from *The Zohar*, Rabbi Isaac and Rabbi Judah meet a young boy as they come upon a vine in a garden. The boy then quotes the verse:

> "Binding his foal to the vine and his ass's colt to the choice vine." He [the young boy] said: 'The word *oseri* (binding) is written here with a superfluous *yod*, and the word '*iro* (his colt) with *hé* instead of *vau*. Thus the Holy Name *Yah* is hinted here. Similarly with the words *bni* (colt) and *sorekah* (choice vine).'[10]

Yah is one of the biblical names of God. You must remember that in Hebrew, there are only consonants. So *Yah* is simply a *yod* and a *hei*. YH is the first part of YHVH, the Tetragramaton, which is translated "LORD" and assumed to be Jehovah although it is never pronounced by Orthodox Jews (they would say *HaShem,* which is Hebrew for "The Name"). A wonderful teaching about *Yah* is found on page 10 in a book by L. Grant Lutton *In His Own Words: Messianic Insights Into The Hebrew Alphabet* (Beth Tikkun Publishing, 1999, available by calling 330-699-9389 or at luton2000@aol.com). Lutton quotes from the Jewish prayerbook, *The Siddur:*

> The first half of the Divine name, formed of the letters *yod* and *hei,* symbolizes the Attribute of Judgment, while the second half, formed of the letters *vav* and *hei,* symbolizes the Attribute of Mercy. The blend of both attributes leads to his desired goal for Creation.

Lutton goes on to say: "This reminds us of Zechariah's words that someday 'YHVH will be King over the whole earth. On that day there will be one YHVH and His name one.' Zech. 14:9."

I truly believe that Genesis 49:10-11 tells us that Shiloh, the Messiah, would bind His foal, the one he rode on into Jerusalem in triumph, to the vine and would wash His clothes in a winepress. This will be developed in more depth later.

The great Jewish commentator Rashi points out that the Hebrew word *suth* translated in Genesis 49:11 as clothes ("and his clothes in the blood of grapes"): "denotes a kind of vesture, but there is no other example of the word in scripture."[11] (Emphasis added.)

I would refer the reader to Bullinger's "Number in Scripture" pages 70-86 to read of the importance of words used only once in Holy Writ. Young's Analytical Concordance (page 174) translates this unusual word suth as "covering." Strong's Concordance translates it as "clothing" but notes that the word #5497 "is probably from the same root as #4533, covering, i.e., clothing.[12]" (Emphasis added.)

This unique word for red clothing suggests Christ's atonement—when we think of our sins being *covered* by the Lord's blood which stained His clothing on that night in the Garden of Gethsemane and issued from His scourged and pierced body on the cross of Calvary. Remember that after the Fall, "the Lord God made coats of skins and clothed them" (Genesis 3:21). While Adam and Eve tried to make their own covering of fig leaves, God clothed them in animal skins which resulted in blood being shed to cover them. This prefigured Christ's shed blood to "cover" our sins.

(2.) The next scripture that tells us about the Messiah in red robes is:

> Who is this that cometh from Edom, with dyed garments from Bozrah? This that is glorious in his apparel, traveling in the greatness of his strength? I that speak in righteousness, mighty to save. Wherefore art thou red in thine apparel, and thy garments like him that treadeth in the winefat? I have trodden the winepress alone; and of the people there was none with me: for I will tread them in mine anger, and trample them in my fury; and their blood shall be sprinkled upon my garments, and I will stain all my raiment. For the day of vengeance is in mine heart, and the year of my redeemed is come. —Isaiah 63:1-3.

If Christ is to appear to the world on the Mount of Olives, why does Isaiah say He will be coming from Edom and Bozrah in red raiment? These biblical places are found today in modern Jordan—in no way mistaken for Mount Olivet. Arnold Fructenbaum's book *The Footsteps of the Messiah*, solved this puzzle for me.

Briefly, Fructenbaum makes a strong case for a righteous remnant of Judah being led out to safety in the End Times like the Hebrew Christians were led to Pella and escaped the wrath of the Romans in 70 A.D. Fructenbaum quotes Zechariah 12: 7:

The Lord also shall save the tents of Judah first, that the glory of the house of David and the glory of the inhabitants of Jerusalem do not magnify themselves against Judah. (Emphasis added.)

Fructenbaum believes the place where the righteous remnant or "tents of Judah" will be led to has to fit four criteria: <u>in the mountains</u>, <u>in the wilderness</u>, <u>a place prepared in advance</u> and <u>someplace very defensible</u>.

His biblical sources for these requirements are as follows: in the mountains: "Then let them that are in Judea flee unto the mountains." Matthew 24:16.

In the wilderness: Fructenbaum notes that in Revelation 12:5-6 Israel is represented as the woman who brought forth a man child (Christ) who was to rule all nations with a rod of iron. "Israel is pictured as a woman; a motif taken from the Old Testament concept of Israel as the wife of Jehovah," he writes.

The wilderness refuge is explained as:

And the woman fled into the wilderness, where she hath a place prepared of God, that they should feed her there a thousand two hundred and threescore days.— Revelation 12:6.

(Note that the timing, 1,260 days, fits the last half of the Tribulation— 3 1/2 years. While Satan rages among the nations, this remnant of Judah will be protected by the Lord.)

Dr. Noah W. Hutchings, in his book *25 Messianic Signs in Israel Today*,[13] notes: "Of this time, the prophet Isaiah indicated that a remnant of Israel would be protected in a special place of chambers:"

Come, my people, enter thou into thy chambers, and shut thy doors about thee: hide thyself as it were for a little moment, until the indignation be overpast. For, behold, the Lord cometh out of his place to punish the inhabitants of the earth for their iniquity: the earth also shall disclose her blood, and shall no more cover her slain.—Isaiah 26:20-21

Dr. Hutchings concurs that Petra is likely to be the hiding place. He writes, "Petra was known as a place of refuge—David found refuge here from Saul . . . The following prophecy indicates this city will be a place of refuge for Israel":

O God, thou hast cast us off, thou hast scattered us, thou has been displeased; O turn thyself to us again . . . Who will bring me into the strong city? who will lead me into Edom? Wilt not thou, O God, which hadst cast us off? and thou, O God, which didst not go out with our armies? Give us help from trouble: for vain is the help of man. Through God we shall do valiantly: for he it is that shall tread down our enemies.—Psalm 60:9-12. (Emphasis added.)

The "escaped of Israel" (Isaiah 10:20-23; 4:2; 37:31-32) shall go to a place prepared in advance that is very defensible as Isaiah 33:16 explains: "his defense shall be the munitions of rocks; his bread shall be given him; his waters shall be sure." Just as the Children of Israel were given manna and water while they sojourned in the wilderness, God will miraculously provide sustenance to this "led-out" remnant of Israel.

Fructenbaum opened up my thinking to consider yet another scriptural reference that may have a bearing on the "tents of Judah" hiding in Petra.

First you need to know that *Petra* is Greek for "rock" and *Sela* is the Hebrew word for "rock." If you have seen pictures of the magnificent buildings the Nabateans carved from towering red rock, canyon walls, you understand immediately why they named their city "rock." The reference we will investigate now is Isaiah 16:1, 4-5:

> Send ye <u>the lamb</u> to the ruler of the land from Sela to the wilderness, unto the mount of the daughter of Zion.
> Let mine outcasts dwell with thee, Moab; be thou a covert to them from the face of the spoiler; for the extortioner is at an end, the spoiler ceaseth, the oppressors are consumed out of the land.
>
> And in mercy shall the throne be established: and he shall sit upon it in truth in the tabernacle of David, judging, and seeking judgment, and hasting righteousness. (Emphasis added.)

In Adam Clarke's commentary (Vol. 4, page 88) he strains to explain why <u>a lamb</u> should be sent to this land of Israel's enemies.

Perhaps this verse refers to the "Lamb of God" going to save the outcasts of Israel who have fled Jerusalem. The land of Moab is where Petra is located. Certainly no king of Israel has yet been able to establish a throne of mercy. In light of the role this place will play in the End Times, it seems to fit the other verses explaining Petra as a place of refuge, a "covert to them from the face of the spoiler."

Citing Daniel 11:41, Fructenbaum explains how the Antichrist will conquer the whole world with the exception of three places.

> He shall enter also into the glorious land, and many countries shall be overthrown: but these shall escape out of his hand, even Edom and Moab and the children of Ammon.

Then Fructenbaum writes:

> All three of these ancient nations currently comprise the
> single modern state of Jordan. The city of Bozrah in
> Mount Seir is located in ancient Edom or southern
> Jordan. Since this area will escape the domination of the
> Antichrist, it is logical for the Jews to flee to this place.
> Thus, God will provide a city of refuge outside the
> Antichrist's domain for the fleeing remnant. It will be a
> very defensible city located in Mount Seir.

Fructenbaum continues:

> The ancient city of Bozrah was located in the region of
> Mount Seir. . . a real fascinating issue is the exact location
> of Bozrah in the mountain range of Mount Seir. Two
> places have been suggested. One is the present Arab village
> of Buseira, which seems to retain the name of Bozrah. The
> other is the city now known as Petra. While both cities
> meet all the above requirements, this author prefers the
> identification with Petra. Petra is located in a basin within
> Mount Seir, and is totally surrounded by mountains and
> cliffs. The only way in and out of the city is through a
> narrow passageway that extends for about a mile and can
> only be negotiated by foot or by horseback. This makes
> the city easy to defend, and its surrounding high cliffs give
> added meaning and confirmation to Isaiah 33:16 ['his
> place of defense shall be the munitions of rocks; his bread
> shall be given him; his waters shall be sure'].[14]

You may wonder at "his waters shall be sure" if you have ever been
anywhere near this desolate wilderness. But archaeologist Nelson Glueck

(in *The Other Side of the Jordan*) studied the carefully terraced hills that were once irrigated by a large spring-fed reservoir and believed this territory could again support a population of several millions, just as it did in the time of the Nabateans, a nomadic Arab people who conquered this area in about 300 B.C.

One of the Nabateans' most prized accomplishments was the system of cisterns including *Um al Biyara*, which is Arabic for "Mother of Cisterns." The Greek historian Diodorus Siculus (80 B.C.-15 B.C.) wrote about this water system: "Their country, without water, is unpenetrable to enemies, but the Nabateans possess cisterns to collect rain water, the place of which is known only to the inhabitants of the country."

Evangelical author Chuck Missler writes:

> Bozrah means 'sheepfold.' An ancient sheepfold had a narrow entrance so that the shepherd could count his sheep, and, once inside, he could guard a single entrance to contain them. (Compare 'I am the door,' John 10.)
>
> It appears that . . . Petra, fits that description, shaped like an ancient sheepfold, with a narrow passageway (the 'Siq') opening up to a spacious city surrounded by cliffs.[15]

Best-selling Christian author Hal Lindsey also concurs about Petra being the place of safety for the "tents of Judah" or the righteous remnant: "The Lord Messiah Jesus will supernaturally protect those who cling to His Word. I believe Petra will be the place of that protection."[16]

If you saw the movie *Indiana Jones and the Last Crusade*, you saw Harrison Ford and Sean Connery at Petra—the lost city with its steep red walls. A very defensible fortress indeed!

As Satan's plan has always been to destroy Israel to thwart the word of God, before the great convergence on Jerusalem by the armies of the earth an attempt will be made to kill this remnant hiding in the safety of a "sheepfold" at Bozrah. But the gentle "Good Shepherd" of Israel is also the fierce "Lion of Judah" and He will save this flock, hence Isaiah's noting His coming from Edom and Bozrah.

I love the following scripture and it is my dearest wish to be enfolded in safety in one of the Holy One of Israel's sheepfolds!

> I will surely assemble, O Jacob, all of thee: I will surely gather the remnant of Israel; I will put them together as <u>the sheep of Bozrah</u>, as a flock in the midst of their pasture; they shall make a great noise by reason of the multitude of men."—Micah 2:12 (emphasis added).

Chuck Missler's tape commentary *The Next Holocaust and the Refuge in Edom* reminds us to consider Isaiah 34:6, 8:

> The sword of the Lord is filled with blood, it is made fat with fatness, and with the blood of lambs and goats, with the fat of the kidneys of rams: for the Lord hath a sacrifice in Bozrah, and a great slaughter in the land of Idumea . . . For it is the day of the Lord's vengeance, and the year of recompenses for the controversy of the Lord.

This verse seems to point to the Day of Vengeance beginning at Edom when the Lord comes to save the "tents of Judah" or the righteous remnant in hiding at Petra.

Deborah and Barak sang a song of praise to the Lord in Judges 5:4-5 which may have a double application: deliverance from the Canaanites and in the end-times from the armies gathered by the Antichrist:

> Lord, when thou wentest out from <u>Seir</u>, when thou marchest out of the field of <u>Edom</u>, the earth trembled, and the heavens dropped, the clouds also dropped water. The mountains melted from before the Lord, even that Sinai from before the Lord God of Israel." (Emphasis added.)

This scripture reminds me of Psalms 68:8 where it says:

> The earth shook, the heavens also dropped at the presence
> of God: even Sinai itself was moved at the presence of
> God, the God of Israel.

Isaiah comments on the warfare of the End Times and ties red-stained garments to massive shedding of blood when he writes:

> For every battle of the warrior is with confused noise, and
> garments rolled in blood; but this shall be with burning
> and fuel of fire. —Isaiah 9:5 (emphasis added.)

Nahum 2:3 makes a similar observation: "The shield of his mighty men is made red, the valiant men are in scarlet." I especially appreciate George M. Lamsa's discussion of red:

> Red is the symbol of blood, and the red horse [of Rev. 6:4]
> symbolizes great destruction of life. The king's bodyguards
> wore scarlet clothes, indicating that they were ready to
> shed blood and to die, if necessary, for their ruler.[17]

What a powerful description of Christ as the warrior arrayed in red, showing that He *did* die to carry out the work given Him by the Father!

I highly recommend Lindsey's *A Prophetical Walk Through the Holy Land*, Fructenbaum's *The Footsteps of the Messiah* and the excellent two-tape commentary by Chuck Missler. (See appendix for more information.)

(3.) And the last scripture that speaks of the clothing stained red from the winepress is yet another judgment verse:

> And he was clothed with a vesture dipped in blood: and his name is called The Word of God. . . And out of his mouth goeth a sharp sword, that with it he should smite the nations: and he shall rule them with a rod of iron: and he treadeth the winepress of the fierceness and wrath of Almighty God.—Revelation 19:13, 15.

This verse is clearly at the time of Christ's Second Coming because the chapter tells of Christ coming on a white horse with the armies of heaven "to smite the nations," to destroy the beast, the false prophet and the armies of the kings of the earth.

The Vine, the Cup and Winepress in Scripture

Lest we think that wine and winepresses refer only to judgment, this is probably an appropriate place to talk about the two-fold nature of wine symbols in scripture. The master of Jewish symbolism, E.R. Goodenough, writes:

> Judaism, like Christianity, never reduced the wine symbols to a single one: wine could be represented as the vine, the cluster of grapes, the cup, a wine jar, baskets of grapes, vintage scenes, and the wine press.[18]

The Vine and a Cup of Blessing

There are traditions that it was the fruit of the vine that Adam and Eve partook of in the Garden of Eden.[19] In the Greek *Third Baruch*, Noah is reluctant to plant the vine following the flood since "Adam was destroyed by it." An angel appears and tells him: "Rise, Noah, plant the sprig, for the Lord says this: 'Its bitterness will be changed into sweetness, and its curse will become a blessing, and its fruit will become the blood of God.' "[20]

A similar Jewish tradition is found in *Bereshith Rabbah* 15, 8 and in *The Zohar* that the fruit in the Garden of Eden was the grape.

Again, it has been said, that one who dreams that he has eaten black grapes can be certain that he will enter the world to come. Why? The clue is to be found in the tradition that the forbidden fruit which was eaten by Adam and Eve was the grape, the fruit of vine, for it is written: 'their grapes are grapes of gall' (Deut. 32:32)—namely the black grapes.[21]

The Catholic scholar Calmet seemed to understand the significance of the vine as an important symbol for in his *Dictionary of the Holy Bible* is the following description of a golden vine:

In the temple at Jerusalem, above and round the gate seventy cubits high, which led from the porch to the holy place, a richly carved vine was extended, as a border and decoration. The branches, tendrils and leaves, were of the finest gold; the stalks of the branches were of the length of the human form, and the bunches hanging upon them were of costly jewels. Herod first placed it there; rich and patriotic Jews from time to time added to its embellishment, one contributing a new grape, another a leaf, and a third even a bunch of the same precious materials. If to compute its value at more than 12,000,000 of dollars be an exaggeration, it is nevertheless indisputable, that this vine must have had an uncommon importance and a sacred meaning in the eyes of the Jews. With what majestic splendor must it likewise have appeared in the evening when it was illuminated by tapers!

If, then, Jesus in the evening, after having celebrated the Passover, again betook himself to the temple with his disciples, what is more natural, than, as they wandered to and fro, that above every thing this vine blazing with gold and jewels should have attracted their attention? that rivetted (sic) by the gorgeous magnificence of the sight, they were absorbed in wonder and contemplation respecting the real import of this work of art? Let us now conceive, that Jesus at this moment, referring to this vine, said to his disciples, 'I am the true vine'—how correct and striking must his words then have appeared!—how clearly and determinately must then the import of them have been seen![22]

It seems very possible to me that this very scene might be described in John 15:1 when Christ said: "I am the true vine, and my Father is the husbandman." Then in verse 5, He repeated these words as if to be sure we understood Him: "I am the vine, ye are the branches: He that abideth in me, and I in Him, the same bringeth forth much fruit: for without me ye can do nothing."

Other positive scriptural accounts using wine or grapes as a metaphor include when Abraham went to King Melchizedek to pay his tithes and was offered bread and wine (Genesis 14:18) in a foreshadowing of the sacramental meal to come.

The Good Samaritan of Luke 10:34 dressed the beaten man's wounds with wine and oil. Wine was tithed (Deuteronomy 14:23) and offered upon the altar ("And for a drink offering thou shalt offer the third part of an hin of wine, for a sweet savor unto the Lord." Numbers 15:7).

Christ's first miracle was to turn water to wine. And there is simply no sweeter metaphor about the great gifts of Jesus than the "Cup of Salvation" or the "Cup of Blessing" that He offers us. Luke 22:17-18, 20 describes the Last Supper:

And he took the cup, and gave thanks, and said, Take this, and divide it among yourselves: For I say unto you, I will not drink of the fruit of the vine, until the kingdom of

God shall come. . . This cup is the new testament in my
blood, which is shed for you."

Paul also writes of this saying: "The cup of blessing which we bless, is
it not the communion of the blood of Christ?" 1 Cor. 10:16.

Rabbi Hayim Halevy Donin emphasizes the significance of wine in
Jewish ritual and life:

> The only fruit that merits a blessing of its own is grape
> juice or wine, the fermented juice of the grape. The
> blessing concludes with: borei pri hagafen ('who creates
> the fruit of the vine'). The fermented juice of other fruits
> or vegetables, even if called 'wine,' does not qualify for this
> blessing. . . Wine as a symbol of joy and celebration was
> given halakhic status when the sages required that
> drinking a cup of wine accompany certain prayers or
> ceremonies. And so a blessing for wine is added to
> Kiddush [said at the beginning of Shabbat], Havdalah [at
> the close of Shabbat], the Rite of Circumcision, the
> Redemption of the First-Born, the Ceremony of Betrothal
> and the Marriage Blessings. Wine, popularly referred to in
> halakhic literature as a 'Cup of Blessing,' plays a key role
> in the seder ritual [for Passover], and is also utilized in the
> Grace After Meals, when said by a quorum.[23]

The Cairo Genizah (a storage place for the sacred records of the Jews
that are worn or damaged) yielded up a treasure trove of long-lost texts in
1896. Along with a copy of a Dead Sea document, was an ancient
forerunner to the blessing on wine mentioned by Rabbi Donin:

Blessed art Thou, O Lord, our God, King of the Universe
who created sweet wine, good must from grapevines,
that is pleasing to a person and good for man,
that gladdens the heart and makes the face shine.

It is a consolation to mourners, and those of bitter spirit forget their misery.

It is medicine to all who drink it (to him who drinks it sensibly)
It is heart's joy, gladness and great delight to its drinkers.
He, our God, created it of old for pleasure,
among the works established from the beginning,
so that all who drink it shall bless God,
and praise the Author of understanding,
who prepared the delicacies of the world,
and formed the sweet things of the earth.[24]

The Cup of Trembling

Yet wine also provides us with the fiercest picture we will get about judgment. Duality of scriptural types can make us comprehend how the Coming of the Lord will be both "great" and "dreadful" depending on whether or not we come to know God through His Son, Jesus of Nazareth!

As beautiful as the images are of the Cup of Salvation that Christ offers us, the "Cup of Trembling" invokes terror, for it signifies the "wrath of God." Psalm 75:8 tells us:

> For in the hand of the Lord there is a cup, and the wine is red; it is full of mixture; and he poureth out of the same: but the dregs thereof, all the wicked of the earth shall wring them out and drink them.

Jeremiah 25: 15, 30-31 continues with this imagery:

> For thus saith the Lord God of Israel unto me; Take the
> wine cup of the fury at my hand, and cause all the nations,
> to whom I send thee, to drink it. . . Therefore prophesy
> thou against them all these words, and say unto them, The
> Lord shall roar from on high, and utter his voice from his
> holy habitation; he shall mightily roar upon his
> habitation; he shall give a shout, as they that tread the
> grapes, against all the inhabitants of the earth. A noise
> shall come even to the ends of the earth; for the Lord hath
> a controversy with the nations, he will plead with all flesh;
> he will give them that are wicked to the sword, saith the
> Lord. (Emphasis added)

Isaiah 51:22-23 notes that God's chosen people Israel will at last find
sorrow and mourning turned away and their wicked oppressors will drink
of the Cup of Trembling:

> Thus saith thy Lord the LORD, and thy God that
> pleadeth the cause of his people, Behold, I have taken out
> of thine hand the cup of trembling, even the dregs of the
> cup of my fury; thou shalt no more drink it again: But I
> will put it into the hands of them that afflict thee; which
> have said to thy soul, Bow down, that we may go over: and
> thou hast laid thy body as the ground, and as the street, to
> them that went over.

As to where the nations will have to drink this wine of God's wrath, the
Lord is very specific. Joel 3:12-13 tells us:

Let the heathen be wakened, and come up to the valley of Jehoshaphat: for there I will sit to judge all the heathen round about. Put ye in the sickle, for the harvest is ripe: come, get you down; for the press is full, the fats overflow; for their wickedness is great.

Smith's Bible Dictionary tells us that "Jehoshaphat" means "Jehovah's judgment" and then notes:

The scene of 'Jehovah's judgment' has been localized, and the name has come down to us attached to that deep ravine which separates Jerusalem from the Mount of Olives, through which at one time the Kedron forced its stream. There is no trace of it in the Bible or in Josephus. In both the only name used for this gorge is Kidron (N.T. Cedron). We first encounter its new title in the middle of the 4th century in the Onomasticon of Eusebius and Jerome, and in the commentary of the latter Father on Joel. Since that time the name has been recognized and adopted by travellers of all ages and all faiths.[25]

Revelation chapter 14 reveals that the wicked and foolish who received the mark of the beast in their forehead or in their hand, will "drink of the wine of the wrath of God, which is poured out without mixture [not tempered with grace by the addition of a small amount of water] into the cup of his indignation; and he shall be tormented with fire and brimstone in the presence of the holy angels, and in the presence of the Lamb" (verse 10).

Then John the Revelator is shown the truly horrifying image of the Winepress of the Lord's Indignation:

And another angel came out from the altar, which had power over fire; and cried with a loud cry to him that had the sharp sickle, saying, Thrust in thy sharp sickle, and gather the clusters of the vine of the earth; for her grapes are fully ripe. And the angel thrust in his sickle into the earth, and gathered the vine of the earth and cast it into the great winepress of the wrath of God. And the winepress was trodden without the city, and the blood came out of the winepress, even unto the horse bridles, by the space of a thousand and six hundred furlongs (Revelation 14:18-20).

Hal Lindsey displays a map picturing Israel in his *A Prophetical Walk Through the Holy Land* and writes of this prophecy from the Book of Revelation:

The map shows the only continuous valley of that length [a thousand and six hundred furlongs or 200 miles] in Israel. It is the Jordan River Valley, which extends southward from the southern end of the Sea of Galilee through the Dead Sea and dried-up river bed called the Wadi al-Arabah, to the Gulf of Eilat (or Aqabah). The fiercest fighting will take place around Jerusalem and along the Jordan Valley. Man will bring such horrible carnage upon himself that blood will stand to the horses' bridles along this Jordan Valley, most of which is below sea level.[26]

Making Wine in the Time of Christ

To begin with, I believe that the subject of wine in scripture can yield much hidden meaning. We might take note of a mystical interpretation regarding wine. Because Hebrew letters also have a numerical value (*aleph*=1, *bet*=2, etc.) words that have the same numerical value are often studied for deeper meanings. This is called *gematria*.

Ancient winepress located within the gardens at the Garden Tomb in Jerusalem

The numerical value of the Hebrew word for wine, *yayin*, is 70 (*yod*=10, *yod*=10, *nun*=50) as is the word for secret, *sod* (*samech*=60, *vav*=6, *dalet*=4). I agree that wine has a great hidden truth, kept secret from casual eyes and hearts.

A midrash teaches: "When the wine enters, the secret (*sod*) comes out."[27] It is my belief that this midrash has explained the connection in too superficial a manner. I believe that wine as a topic has much more to offer regarding secrets than merely loosening one's tongue. Wine has hidden deep mysteries such as what we learned about wine and milk in the previous chapter and what I will present regarding the winepress in this chapter.

It is now time to consider what ancient winemaking in the time of the Bible can teach us. Wine was made in a winepress that was often carved out of rock with two vats connected by a trough, one vat higher than the other. The grapes were placed in the upper of the two vats and were then trodden on by the winetreaders, causing the juice to flow into the lower vat.

Corn, wine and oil are noted in Deuteronomy 14:23 as being tithed. Only the very best was given as a tithe to the Lord at His holy Temple. Fausset's *Bible Cyclopaedia Critical and Expository* observes on page 723: "The first drops ('the tear,' *dema*, marg. Exod. 22:29) were consecrated as firstfruits to Jehovah." The verse where Fausset remarks parenthetically on the word "tear" (like a "teardrop") reads: "Thou shalt not delay to offer the first of thy ripe fruits, and of thy liquors. . ." Where you read 'liquors' the Hebrew word is *dema* which means tear and this is the only use of the word in the Hebrew Bible.

The 1881 *Comprehensive and Explanatory Bible Encyclopaedia* edited by Edward Robinson, D.D. LL.D, notes: "The Wine of Libation (Deut.

32:38, Esther 9:17) was the most excellent wine, poured on the victims in the temple of the Lord."

And how was this "first wine," consecrated to the Lord, obtained? Smith's Dictionary of the Bible notes that: "a certain amount of juice exuded from the ripe fruit from its own pressure before the treading commenced. This appears to have been kept separate from the rest of the juice, and to have formed the 'sweet wine' noticed in Acts 2:13." Botanists Harold N. and Alma L. Moldenke confirm this in their writing on wine:

> The fresh grapes were dumped into the upper vat (Hebrew for 'winevat' is '*begat*'). A certain amount of juice exuded naturally into the lower vat just as a result of the weight of the grapes upon each other. This was the juice of the ripest and softest of the grapes, and was carefully gathered and kept separate from the juice later pressed out. It was the 'sweet wine' (Hebrew '*tirosh*'), 'new wine' (Hebrew, '*ahsis*'), or 'first wine' of Hosea 4:11, Amos 9:13 and Acts 2:13. After this had been gathered, the pressing of the grapes began through the age-old process of 'treading.[28]

One of my dearest friends from high school, Dave Tuttle, told me that he and his wife Billie have raised grapes and could understand this "first" wine process from their experience in making grape juice. He wrote to me about this "first wine" that is the result of the grapes' weight pressing down: "I thought of this being like 'uncompelled wine,' coming forth of its own volition, without compulsory means, as the dew from heaven. What a tender, yet powerful view of the Savior's sweet willingness."

In Jewish writings about the Red Heifer, it is noted that the heifer must go to the Mount of Olives willingly. In the Mishnah tractate about the Red Heifer it notes that "If the [red] heifer would not go forth, she was not to be led out with a black [heifer] so that none may say, They slaughtered a black [heifer] and not a red one, nor [may they send out with her another] red [heifer] lest they say, They slaughtered two [red heifers]."[29] This type of utter willingness is fulfilled in Christ's words from John 10:15, 17-18:

> As the Father knoweth me, even so know I the Father: and I lay down my life for the sheep. . . Therefore doth my Father love me, because I lay down my life, that I might take it up again. <u>No man taketh it from me</u>, but I lay it down, and I have power to take it again. This commandment have I received of the Father. (Emphasis added.)

Getting back to the ancient wine maker—he knew he must tithe his crop. He would take the most choice grapes from his vineyard. These he would carefully place in the winepress. But no one would touch them! The weight of the grapes would press down and bruise those beneath until a small amount of choice wine would extrude—the "tear," like a tear drop. After the consecrated wine was collected, the vintage would continue with men then leaping in the winepress to stomp out the rest of the wine.

Knowing that wine was made in two separate stages opens up the way for us to interpret the winepress scriptures as two images: one of mercy and one of judgment.

The Messiah of the Winepress

Spurgeon puzzled over Isaiah 63:1-2 with an entire sermon devoted to it on February 13, 1887: "Who Is This?"

> Who is this that cometh from Edom, with dyed garments from Bozrah? This that is glorious in his apparel, traveling in the greatness of his strength? I that speak in righteousness, mighty to save. Wherefore art thou red in thine apparel, and thy garments like him that treadeth in the winefat? I have trodden the winepress alone; and of the

people there was none with me: for I will tread them in mine anger, and trample them in my fury; and their blood shall be sprinkled upon my garments, and I will stain all my raiment. For the day of vengeance is in mine heart, and the year of my redeemed is come. —Isaiah 63:1-3.

First, he recognizes the judgment aspect of this verse:

What astonishment there will be among the sons of men when He shall appear in His vesture dipped in blood, smiting the nations with His iron rod—yea, dashing them in pieces as potters' vessels! In those last tremendous times, when the day of vengeance shall have arrived, then shall the winepress be trodden without [outside of] the city, even the great winepress of the wrath of God. No tongue can fully tell of the terrors of that day when our Lord shall say, 'Ah, I will ease me of mine adversaries.' While He shall give victory to the cause of peace, and purity, and truth, and righteousness, and shall save all those who believe in Him, <u>He shall bruise Satan under His feet, and crush the powers of darkness</u>. (Emphasis added.)[30]

Can you see Christ treading on His enemies, putting all things under His feet and crushing the head of the serpent that once bruised His heel? (See Genesis 3:15.)

But Spurgeon also saw in this verse reference to the Lord's passion—or the suffering He undertook in His great work of redemption: first in the Garden of Gethsemane, then during His scourging and crucifixion. Spurgeon wrote:

The church by a holy instinct has referred the passage to our Lord's first as well as His second coming, and she has not been in error. . . The passage is poetical: the battle is a spiritual one; the conflict is with sin and with the powers of darkness; and the conqueror returns from the fight having utterly destroyed his foes, of which his blood-dyed garments are the surest evidence. . . I mean so to use this passage this morning, with a consciousness that I am not accommodating it, nor taking it from its natural sense at all; but rather placing it in the light of <u>its first great fulfillment</u>. I have not concealed from you its relation to the Second Advent, when the Lord Jesus shall appear in victory 'clothed with a vesture dipped in blood'; but at the same time this is a picture of salvation rather than destruction, and its hero appears as 'mighty to save,' in fulfillment of a divine proclamation: "Behold, thy salvation cometh." (Emphasis added.)[31]

E.W. Bullinger studied Isaiah 63:1-2 and found reason to disagree strongly with Spurgeon's first coming fulfillment:

The whole scene is one of judgment and of vengeance (compare Isaiah 9:5). How any could ever understand this as referring to, or foretelling, the Redeemer's sufferings in grace, we cannot imagine. No! . . . The rider on the white horse is not the Gracious Saviour in His work of saving His people from their sins; but the Righteous Judge who avenges them on their enemies.[32]

Would that Spurgeon and Bullinger had understood that first reference in Genesis 49:11 about Shiloh's clothing stained with wine—it fits beautifully with Spurgeon's belief that the winepress referred to salvation as well as judgment. If we were to think of this verse as relating to Christ in the Garden of Gethsemane as if He were the precious fruit placed in the winepress—remember that Paul testified: "But now is Christ risen from the dead, and become the *firstfruits* of them that slept" I Cor. 15:20 (emphasis added)—could not His blood pressed out by the very weight of the Atonement, be part of His consecrated offering to God? I suggest that those silent drops of blood that fell in the Garden of Gethsemane were *teardrops of mercy* that Christ bled for us.

Could it be that the three winepress scriptures are signifying: (1) the Winepress of Mercy in the Garden of Gethsemane, (2) the Winepress of Judgment against those who try to annihilate the "tents of Judah" at Bozrah and (3) the Winepress of Judgment against the armies of the world surrounding Jerusalem and gathered down through the Valley of Jehoshaphat that runs between the city walls of Jerusalem and the Mount of Olives?

More on Christ's Suffering in Gethsemane

There is another voice to join the song of praise for our Savior's work in Gethsemane. A.W. Pink suggests yet another grief to be overcome in the Garden of Gethsemane—that of the wrath of God. Pink wrote in *The Seven Sayings of the Saviour on the Cross*:

> Then cometh Jesus with them unto a place called Gethsemane, and saith unto the disciples, Sit ye here while I go and pray yonder. And he took with Him, Peter, and the two sons of Zebedee, and began to be sorrowful and very heavy. Then saith He unto them, 'My soul is exceeding sorrowful, even unto death: tarry ye here, and watch with Me.' And He went a little farther, and fell on His face, and prayed, saying, 'O My Father, if it be possible, let this cup pass from Me: nevertheless not as I will, but as Thou wilt.' (Matt. 26:36-39). Here He views the black clouds arising. He sees the dreadful storm coming, He premeditated the inexpressible horrors of that three hours darkness and all they held [the time on the cross

when the Father withdrew His spirit from Christ]. 'My soul is exceeding sorrowful' He cries. The Greek is most emphatic. He was begirt with sorrow. He was plunged over head and ears in the anticipated wrath of God. All the faculties and powers of His soul were wrung with anguish. St. Mark employs another form of expression—'He began to be sore amazed' (14:33). The original signifies the greatest extremity of amazement, such as makes one's hair stand on end and their flesh to creep. And, Mark adds, 'and to be very heavy,' which denotes there was an utter sinking of spirit; His heart was melted like wax at the sight of the terrible Cup. But the evangelist Luke uses the strongest terms of all: 'And being in an agony He prayed more earnestly: and His sweat was as it were great drops of blood falling down to the ground' (Luke 22:24). The Greek word for 'agony' here means to be engaged in a combat. Before, He had combated the oppositions of men and the oppositions of the Devil, but now He faces the cup which God gives Him to drink. It was the cup which contained *the undiluted wrath of a sin-hating God.*

Pink continues regarding Christ's agony in the garden:

He shed blood—just like great beads of water in ordinary cases. And here we see the fitness of the place chosen to be the scene of this terrible but preliminary suffering. 'Gethsemane'—ah, thy name betrayeth thee! It means the olive-press. It was the place where the life-blood of the olives was pressed out drop by drop! The chosen place was well named then. It was indeed a fitting footstool to the Cross, a footstool of agony unutterable and unparalleled. On the cross then, Christ drained the Cup which was presented to Him in Gethsemane.[33]

Alfred Edersheim also wrote about the agony in the Garden of Eden:

> But what, may we reverently ask, was the cause of this sorrow unto death of the Lord Jesus Christ? Not fear, either of bodily or mental suffering: but Death. . . No one as He could know what Death was (not dying, which men dread, but Christ dreaded not); no one could taste its bitterness as He. His going into Death was His final conflict with Satan for man, and on his behalf. By submitting to it He took away the power of Death; He disarmed Death by burying his shaft in His own heart. And beyond this lies the deep, unutterable mystery of Christ bearing the penalty due to our sin, bearing our death, bearing the penalty of the broken Law, the accumulated guilt of humanity, and the holy wrath of the Righteous Judge upon them.[34]

And the Lutheran preacher, Joseph A. Seiss (1832-1904) wrote:

> We know something of the wrestling and agony which our Saviour suffered in the Garden of Gethsemane. We know how sorrowful was His soul, as though His immortal being were about to be broken up. We know how He was inwardly wrung with anguish until every pore issued sweat of blood, clotting on His body and falling in great drops to the ground. It was 'the hour of the powers of darkness,' as He himself explained. It was an experience of agony the likes of which never had been, and never could be again.[35]

While preparing this book to go to press I found two more thought-provoking quotes about the Savior in the Garden of Gethsemane.

Dutch Sheets, senior pastor of Springs Harvest Fellowship in Colorado Springs, Colorado wrote this:

> Without any question Christ's redemption of humanity—the work of intercession—began with his travail in the Garden. Isaiah prophesied of Him: "He shall see the *travail* of His soul and shall be satisfied" (Isa. 53:11, KJV, italics mine).
>
> In fulfillment of this, Jesus cried out in Gethsemane saying, "My soul is exceeding sorrowful, even unto death" (Matt. 26:38, KJV). It was in the Garden of Gethsemane that redemption began and the victory of the entire ordeal was won.
>
> We know that redemption was beginning in this travail for a couple of reasons. Luke tells us Jesus began to shed great drops of blood. Jesus was not simply sweating so profusely that it was like a person bleeding. He was literally bleeding through the pores of His skin, a medical condition known as hematidrosis. We must understand that when the blood of Christ began to flow, redemption was beginning, for it is through the shedding of His blood that we have the cleansing from sin (see Heb. 9:22).[36]

The second reference comes from Raniero Cantalamessa, a former professor of Ancient Christianity at the Catholic University of Milan. He has written:

> In Jesus, at Gethsemane, the words of Isaiah are completely fulfilled: "Bruised for our iniquities, upon him was the chastisement that made us whole" (Is 53:5). Now the mysterious words of many psalms will come true, like those of Psalm 88: "Your wrath lies heavy upon me, and you overwhelm me with all your waves. . . Your wrath has swept

over me; your dread assaults destroy me." These words suggest the image of an island left desolate and bare by a hurricane. What would happen if the whole physical universe with its billions and billions of celestial bodies rested on only one point, like an immense, overturned pyramid? What pressure that point would have to bear! Well then, the whole moral universe of sin, no less boundless than the physical universe, weighed on the soul of Jesus at that moment.[37]

Throughout the Bible we are given two images of the blessed Messiah: the spotless Lamb of God whose precious blood redeems us and the mighty Lion of Judah who will cleanse the earth of wickedness with the brightness of His Second Coming. He came to offer Himself as the Suffering Servant in love and He will yet come as the Triumphant King to save His faithful ones and judge a wicked earth as the conquering Lion of Judah.

Can you see Messianic implications in the prophecy that in the Millennium, the enmity of the animals shall cease and the lamb shall lie down with the lion, the kid with the wolf, etc. (Isaiah 11:6)? In that Millennial day, following the cleansing of the earth the judgment and mercy of Christ's nature will be perfectly balanced and He will then have a people and a place worthy of Him.

Jesus Christ came the first time to offer us His mercy. He trod the winepress alone. Or we might say *He allowed Himself* to be trodden by sin, death and the wrath of God in the Winepress of Mercy. He alone bore the weight of the sins of the world and paid the price of the wrath of God against sinners. He was "bruised" under the fierce weight of our iniquities and the wrath of a Righteous God. Yet it pleased the Father to bruise Him. With the stripes of His scourging we are healed. By the piercing and pouring out of His blood on the Cross of Calvary we find new life.

We begin to understand the physical pain and spiritual grief that Christ endured. Perhaps now we can truly understand how Isaiah 53:11 was foretelling what Christ would suffer in His soul:

He shall see the travail of his soul and shall be satisfied: by
his knowledge shall my righteous servant justify many; for
he shall bear their iniquities.

No wonder the Father would say, "This is my beloved Son, in whom I
am well pleased" (Matthew 3:17). As Max Lucado writes, "No wonder
they call Him Savior!"

"He Was Bruised for Our Iniquities"

A study of the Hebrew word for "bruise" uncovers a scriptural
connection between the suffering of the Lord Jesus Christ and the
(admittedly lesser!) painful experiences His followers undergo in
mortality. There is a reason this mortal life is called "a vale of tears." Christ
even told us in John 16:33: ". . . In the world ye shall have tribulation: but
be of good cheer; I have overcome the world." (Emphasis added.)

The Hebrew word for bruise is "*daka*" (in Strong's, *daka* is #1792 and
#1793, which have the same Hebrew letters, but are "pointed" differently,
i.e., slightly different vowels are supplied for the Hebrew letters *dalet, kaf,
aleph*). *Daka* is translated as "bruised" only in "The Suffering Servant"
Isaiah chapter 53, verses 5 and 10: "he was bruised for our iniquities" and
"Yet it pleased the Lord to bruise him."

In Wilson's *Old Testament Word Studies* (page 57) he writes of this word
daka: "to bruise, break in small pieces; to smite; applied to the mind, and used
of the Messiah, it designates the most severe inward and outward suffering."

A shorter form of this word: "*dak*" is used three times in the Psalms
(and nowhere else) and is translated as "oppressed." When you look up
oppressed in Young's Concordance (page 721) *dak* is translated as
"bruised, oppressed." So when you read in Psalms 9:9 "The Lord also will
be a refuge for the oppressed, a refuge in times of trouble," and in Psalms
10:18 when God is implored "To judge the fatherless and the oppressed,
that the man of the earth may no more oppress" and again in Psalms
74:21 "O let not the oppressed return ashamed: let the poor and needy

praise thy name"—know that the bruised and lowly of this earth are lifted up by the bruising that our Lord suffered for us.

But *daka* is found 19 times in all in the Hebrew Bible (which suggests to me the Red Heifer of Numbers 19). It is used as: bruised, beat, broken, contrite, crush, destroy, humble, oppress and smitten. (Nine different ways this word is used; Bullinger notes that nine is the number of judgment.) There are two verses that use the Hebrew word *daka* as "contrite" and make the beautiful connection of us being "crushed" in a similar manner as our Savior was:

> The Lord is nigh unto them that are of a broken heart; and saveth such as be of a <u>contrite</u> spirit. —Psalms 34:18 (Emphasis added.)

> For thus saith the high and lofty One that inhabiteth eternity, whose name is Holy; I dwell in the high and holy place, with him also that is of a contrite and humble spirit, to revive the spirit of the humble, and to revive the heart of the <u>contrite</u> ones. —Isaiah 57:15 (Emphasis added).

I found a similar Jewish interpretation of the idea of being "crushed" in the writings of the late Rebbe Menachem Schneerson, the revered spiritual leader of the Chabad Lubavitcher sect of Orthodox Jews:

> By virtue of the crushing severity of the current exile, we will ultimately be shown the luminary that lights up the Torah from within. This connection is hinted at in the phrase which specifies that the olive oil for the *Menorah* in the *Mishkan* [Tabernacle] is to be—'*crushed* for *illumination.*' And in this spirit the Sages teach: 'Why have Israel been likened to the olive?—To teach you that just as the olive does not release its oil unless it is crushed,

so too the Jewish people [do not repent except through suffering.]' (Emphasis and brackets in original)[38]

There is one sacrifice that we can offer our Father right now:

For thou desirest not sacrifice; else would I give it: thou delightest not in burnt offering. The sacrifices of God are a broken spirit; a broken and a contrite heart, O God, thou wilt not despise. Psalm 51:16-17

If we have a "crushed" spirit, if we can be as sweetly submissive to the Father's will as Christ was and is, then we will be worthy of being revived and lifted up.

The more you understand about Christ's atonement, the more you are indebted to the Holy One of Israel. The only thanks you can offer is praise. I am indebted to my dear friend Donna Nielsen who found the following versions of Ephesians 3:17-21 in the NLT and NIV:

And I pray that Christ will be more and more at home in your hearts as you trust in him. May your roots go down deep into the soil of God's marvelous love. And may you have power to understand as all saints should, how wide, how long, how high, and how deep his love really is. May you experience the love of Christ, although it is so great you will never fully understand it. Then you will be filled with the fullness of life and power that comes from God.

Now glory be to God! By his mighty power at work within us, he is able to accomplish infinitely more than we would ever dare ask or hope. May he be given glory in the church and in Christ Jesus throughout all generations, for ever and ever! Amen.

"Were You There?"

There is a magnificent painting called "Forgiven" by Thomas Blackshear II. In a book by Roy Lessin featuring this painting is the following description:

> The print features a contemporary man in a pose of despair, ready to fall to the ground. In one hand he has a mallet and in the other a large spike. These are symbols of the truth that each one of us is responsible for Christ's death on the cross. Holding up this broken man is Jesus Christ. The entire scene takes place on Mt. Calvary, the place where His blood was shed. On the ground lilies grow—a powerful reminder that out of death has come new life, the resurrection life of Jesus Christ.[39]

I have tried to do as Thomas Blackshear did, to place myself at one of the scenes of the Lord's suffering. In my mind's eye I can see the Garden of Gethsemane bathed in the cold moonlight of the Passover's full moon. I lug a huge woven basket of my life's sins into the place where the Christ lies prostrate with grief and horror. One by one, all of mankind takes a turn pouring out a burden of evil on His broad shoulders. I add my load, cringing in shame as the sins slide out, each one more horrible to me than the last. And I watch my drop of blood weep its way to the ground, an offering pressed out in the Winepress of Mercy where Christ's blood became the precious offering to God—where He began the Atonement with the voluntary shedding of His precious blood.

Trodden under by all the sins, griefs, woes and iniquities that have and will torment mankind, Christ bled His sinless life's blood to make propitiation. From the dawn of history with Father Adam to the last soul to be born into this world, He took on this burden, suffering these horrors of the soul. As Adam brought death and sin into the world in a garden called Eden, so the Second Adam conquered death and sin beginning in a garden called

Gethsemane and finishing on a Cross without the city walls, rising that first Easter morning in yet another beautiful garden. Isaiah's words ring in my heart:

> All we like sheep have gone astray; we have turned every one to his own way; and the Lord hath <u>laid on him</u> the iniquity of us all. Isaiah 53:6 (Emphasis added).

I know that Spurgeon also considered this scene for he writes of Christ buried under a flood of transgression:

> Sin with many streams had been flowing down the hills of time and forming by their dread accumulation one vast and fathomless lake. Into this the sinner's substitute must be plunged. He had a baptism to be baptized with and He must endure it, or all His chosen must perish forever. That was a day of vengeance when all the waves and billows of divine wrath went over His innocent head.[40]

Spurgeon's words are no doubt echoes of Jonah's:

> For thou has cast me into the deep, in the midst of the seas; and the floods compassed me about: all thy billows and thy waves passed over me." Jonah 2:3.

These sorrowful words are also found in Psalm 42:6-7: O my God, my soul is cast down within me . . . all thy waves and thy billows are gone over me.

Do we wonder any longer why Christ's pure soul shrank from that bitter cup that He knew He had to partake of to the very last dregs? But glory be to God! He finished the work the Father gave Him to do. And you and I can claim His blood to cover us.

Types and Shadows of the Atonement

As we look back on the Sacrifice of the Red Heifer, knowing now what red to white signifies, does it minister to our understanding of just what Christ did for us? As we think of the High Priest standing on the Mount of Olives across the valley from the Holy Temple sprinkling drops of the heifer's blood toward the Holy Place as a sin offering, is there a type in thinking of Jesus with His precious teardrops of blood being offered in a winepress in the Garden of Gethsemane on that same mount? Among those olive groves do we find a teaching about *being* in the winepress and then later *treading* it?

In the 17 years since I first stood on the Mount of Olives I am just beginning to comprehend what Christ suffered so that He could offer His great gift of redemption to the world. As I try to understand just what the Sacrifice of the Red Heifer teaches me about the Holy One of Israel, I can only marvel at the beauty of God's Word.

The Holy Scriptures are indeed like the Master, a source of never-ending waters to refresh the soul and lead us back to our heavenly home. The clues about the Messiah and His redemptive work have been hidden there all along—hidden to reward those who diligently seek and to protect those who would have treated such sacred ideas with disrespect (to their own condemnation).

A spotless Red Heifer offered its lifeblood to cleanse Israel temporarily from death on a mountain where olive groves abound. Madeleine S. Miller would have us consider these words as if spoken by an olive tree in that lonely garden 2,000 years ago:

That night in cool Gethsemane
Christ taught us immortality.
We heard him pray beneath our boughs
And felt his wrestling spirit's vows,
While high upon her ancient hills,
Jerusalem, walled in smugness, slept
Nor guessed that her own Saviour wept
Beyond the Kedron's full spring rills.
We trembled with his lonely woes,
We longed to crash on all his foes,
We saw his face when he arose
— a Conqueror!

So for his sake we cannot die,
But from our gnarled, decrepit root
Send up a new young slender shoot
To tell his victory to the sky.
Before our old self bows to earth,
We give a scion olive birth
To witness what we learned that night
When Christ slew death within our sight
And to our hushed Gethsemane
Entrusted immortality.[41]

One of Judaism's greatest philosophers, Abraham Joshua Heschel, made this wise observation:

> The Bible is a seed, God is the sun, but we are the soil.
> Every generation is expected to bring forth new
> understanding and new realization.[42]

I pray that I have been fertile soil to testify of God's love for us in sending His Only Begotten Son. In testifying that Jesus is the Christ and that He is the only door back to God and that God"s Word is deep and beautiful and full of hidden treasures. I close with the prayer, *Maranatha!* "Come Lord Jesus, Come!"

1. C.H. Spurgeon, *Christ in the Old Testament,* AMG Publishers, 1994, page 464.
2. *A Commentary on the Whole Bible,* edited by J.R. Dummelow, Macmillan and Co., Limited, 1919, page 767.
3. Adam Clarke, *Clarke's Commentary—Matthew-Revelation,* Abingdon, XXXX, page 491.
4. E.W. Bullinger, *Number in Scripture,* Kregel Publications, Grand Rapids, Michigan, 1967, page 108.
5. Henry W. Soltau, *The Tabernacle: The Priesthood and Offerings,* Kregel Publications, 1972, page 118.
6. C.H. Spurgeon, *Christ in the Old Testament,* AMG Publishers, 994, page 464.
7. Harold N. and Alma L. Moldenke, *Plants of the Bible,* Dover Publications, New York, 1952, page 160.
8. Spurgeon, op cited, page 518.
9. Spurgeon, op cited, page 652.
10. *The Zohar,* translated by Harry Sperling, Maurice Simon, The Soncino Press, London, New York, 1984, Vol. II, page 363.
11. (Rashi is an acronym for **Rabbi Solomon ben Isaac**), *Pentateuch with Targum Onkelos, Haphtorah and Rashi's Commentary,* Hebrew Publishing Company, New York, n.d., page 246.
12. *Strong's Exhaustive Concordance of the Bible,* n.d., page 82, Hebrew and Chaldee Dictionary.
13. Dr. Noah W. Hutchings with Gilla Treibich, *25 Messianic Signs in Israel Today,* Hearthstone Publishing Company, Oklahoma City, OK, 1999, page 165.
14. Arnold Fructenbaum, *The Footsteps of the Messiah,* Ariel Ministries Press, 1995, page 204.
15. Chuck Missler, *The Next Holocaust and the Refuge in Edom,* 2 cassette tapes and supplemental notes, Koinonia House, P.O. Box D, Coeur d'Alene, Idaho.
16. Hal Lindsey, *A Prophetical Walk Through the Holy Land,* Harvest House, 1987, page 167.
17. George M. Lamsa, *New Testament Commentary from the Aramaic and the Ancient Eastern Customs,* A.J. Holman Company, 1945, page 565.
18. Erwin R. Goodenough, *Jewish Symbols in the Greco-Roman Period,* Vol. 5, Bollingen Series XXXVII, Pantheon Books, 1956, page 99.
19. Greek *Third Baruch,* edited by James H. Charlesworth, *The Old Testament Pseudepigrapha,* Vol. I, Doubleday & Company, Inc., Garden City, New York, 1983, page 667,
20. Footnote q in the Greek *Third Baruch,* Vol. I, James H. Charlesworth's *The Old Testament Pseudepigrapha,* page 667, notes that "This tree is identified as the vine by second century sages as well: R. Meir (b. Sanh 70a) and R. Judah b. Ilai (GenR 15:7). It is also mentioned in ApAb 23:5 and the *Palea Historica* (ed.Vassiliev, page 190).
21. *The Zohar,* Soncino Press, London, New York, 1983, Vol. IV, page 7.

22. Dom Augustin Calmet, *Calmet's Dictionary of the Holy Bible*, Chatto and Windus, Picadilly, 1875, page 877.
23. Rabbi Hayim Halevy Donin, *To Pray As a Jew*, Basic Books, 1980, page 309.
24. Quoted by Arnold A. Wieder, *Ben Sira and The Praises of Wine*, Jewish Quarterly Review, 61, No. 2, 1970, pages 155-56.
25. *A Dictionary of the Bible*, edited by William Smith, LL.D., Fleming H. Revell Company, n.d., page 277.
26. Hal Lindsey, op cited, pages 196-97.
27. *Numbers Rabbah*, 10; *Tahuma* 8; TB *Eruvin* 65a. (See *Jewish Heritage* on-line magazine: www.jhom.com/topics/wine/gematria.htm).
28. Harold N. and Alma L. Moldenke, *Plants of the Bible*, Dover Publications, Inc. 1986, page 213.
29. *Mishnayoth*, Vol. VI, *Parah*, Judaica Press, Ltd. Gateshead, England, 1983, page 418.
30. C.H. Spurgeon, *Christ in the Old Testament*, AMG Publications, 1994, page 647.
31. Op cited, pages 647-48.
32. E.W. Bullinger, *Commentary on Revelation*, Kregel Publications, 1984, pages 599-600.
33. A.W. Pink, *The Seven Sayings of Christ on the Cross*, Baker Book House, 1992, pages 74-75.
34. Alfred Edersheim, *The Life and Times of Jesus the Messiah*, Vol. II, Wm. B. Eerdmans Publishing Co., 1986, pages 424-25.
34. Joseph A. Seiss, *The Gospel in the Stars*, Kregel Publications, first published 1882, reprinted 1972, page 45.
35. Dutch Sheets, *Intercessory Prayer: How God Can Use Your Prayers to Move Heaven and Earth*, Regal Books, Ventura, California, 1996, page 129.
36. Rainiero Cantalamessa, *Life In Christ: A Spiritual Commentary on the Letter to the Romans*, Vineyard Publishing, Freehold, New Jersey, 1997, page 54.
37. Rabbi Menachem Schneerson, *From Exile to Redemption: Chassidic Teachings of the Lubavitcher Rebbe*, Kehot Publication Society, Brooklyn, NY, 1992, Vol. I, page 41.
38. Forgiven the Painting by Thomas Blackshear II, *Heart Reflections* by Roy Lessin, The Masterpiece Collection, 1996, introduction.
39. C.H. Spurgeon, *Christ in the Old Testament*, AMG Publishers, 1994, (originally published by Passmore and Alabaster in London in 1899), page 464.
40. Madeleine S. and J. Lane Miller, *Encyclopedia of Bible Life*, Harper & Brothers Publishers, 1944, apge 212.
41. Abraham Joshua Heschel, *God in Search of Man: A Philosophy of Judaism*, Noonday, 1955, page 274.

Acknowledgments

I owe much gratitude for family and friends who have supported me and blessed me in my studies: My children Leigh Fullmer (almost a Ph.D.), Dirk Fullmer (with his beautiful wife Jody and grandsons Dallon and Austin), Brooke Boren Ford (and her dear husband Christopher and children Alex and Nicholas) and my encourager Jeremy Boren (the proud daddy of Gage Kalpakoff)—my angel mother Luella Christiansen and sisters Patricia Smith (and her good husband Ron), Linda Tingey and my brother Val Christiansen (and wife Darla).

I am so grateful for friends who supported me in prayer and friendship: Donna Nielsen, Michelle Ainscough, Laura Cook, Patricia Hunter, Margaret Murphy, Glenda Mastin, AliceAnn Crown, Paula Turner and Phyllis Lepard. I am grateful to my sister Pat and to Keith Hepworth for assisting me financially so I could fly to Mississippi to meet the Rev. Clyde Lott and talk with Rabbi Richman again.

I will be forever in the debt of Gene and Carol Rippe who made it possible for me to go on Vendyl Jones's dig at Qumran. Their kindness and patience has meant so much to me. I was also given financial support by Pastor Mahonri Faber, John M. Conrad's congregation, Gerry Avant, Fred Keller, Dina Bassett, John Robbins and many others who sent money after I was on Jack Stockwell's radio program on KTKK in Salt Lake City. May our Blessed God reward you for your kindness.

For technical help I gratefully thank Lynn Rogers and genius Paul Springer. Travis Parry of Grayson's Printing is a miracle worker and does the impossible in unbelievable time.

Also, many thanks to Pam Mayes, Robben Hixson, Jim and Annette Lehman, Bruce K. Smith, David Doane, Craig Rosenberg, Jack and Barbara Kelley, Darrell Perkins, Lori Fiechter (whose magnificent poetry lights my heart), Patrice Hirning, M.D. who ministered to body and soul through some difficult times, Sam Weller (and his extensive bookstore with the used-book religion section that enabled me to build a library on my limited budget), David M. Tuttle for his valuable critiques, Harold Lundstrom for the gift of Adam Clarke's commentary, Jane Sylvester for research, and so many more whose financial help, phone calls, letters and e-mail have encouraged me to continue—may you be blessed as you have blessed me.

To Chuck and Nancy Missler, Rabbi Chaim Richman, Rev. Clyde Lott and Dean Hubbard, Vendyl Jones and Jim Long, deepest gratitude for your tutoring.

And to Teri Williams for following God's lead to financially make this dream come true, my heartfelt thanks.

Appendix

**Contact information for ministries and
newsletters that have been helpful in my studies:**

Church, J.R. monthly magazine *Prophecy in the News,* P. O. Box 7000, Oklahoma City, OK 73153. Office phone: 405-634-1234. Online at: www.prophecyinthenews.com.

Bullinger, E.W. A special ministry to republish the works of Bullinger and provide a Christian newsletter is available at: Truth for Today Bible Fellowship, Joseph L. Watkins, Editor, P. O. Box 6358, Lafayette, IN 47903. Phone: 765-742-2958. Online at: http//tftmin.org. The book on Bible colors by D.L. Higginbotham is also available through this ministry.

Fructenbaum, Arnold The insightful book, *The Footsteps of the Messiah,* is available at Ariel Ministries, P. O. Box 3723, Tustin, CA 92782 in the USA or at P. O. Box 33, Roxboro, H8Y 3E8, Quebec, Canada. Phone: 714-259-4800. Website: http://www.ariel.org.

Jones, Vendyl The Vendyl Jones Research Institutes, P. O. Box 120366, Arlington, TX 76012-0366. Phone: 972-660-6222. Website: www.vendyljones.org.il and e-mail at: vjri@earthlink.net. One of my life goals was to go on an archaeological dig and I pray to be on Vendyl's next dig!

Levitt, Zola is a dedicated supporter of Israel and Messianic teacher. Address: P. O. Box 12268, Dallas, TX 75225-0268. Phone: 214-696-8844. Online at: www.levitt.com.

Lindsey, Hal *Time* magazine heralded Lindsey as the Writer of the Decade in the '70s for his best-seller, *The Late Great Planet Earth.* Lindsey's e-newsletter is well worth checking daily at: oraclenews@hallindseyoracle.com. You can sign up to receive it. He has the best links to European and Israeli news sources, providing information that never gets published in the U.S. Phone: 1-800-TITUS-35. Mail: Oracle House Publishing, Inc., P. O. Box 1131, Murrieta, CA 92564.

Lott, Rev. Clyde 270 Moss Road, Canton, MS 39046.

Meier, Rabbi Levi Ancient Secrets available from Jewish Lights Publishing, P.O. Box 237, Sunset Farm Offices, Rt. 4, Woodstock, VT 05091. Website: www.jewishlights.com

Missler, Chuck I can't think of another single Bible teacher who has taught me as much as Chuck has. I was blessed to go on one of his tours and I took notes nonstop the whole time I was in Israel. I highly recommend Missler's many tapes and books. His wife Nan has a special ministry of her own teaching how to live a true Christian life. I adore this woman! New subscribers get a one-year free subscription to *Personal Update,* an incredible monthly magazine. Contact: Koinonia House, P. O. Box D, Coeur d'Alene, ID 83816-0347. Website: www.khouse.org. PHone: 208-773-6310. I bless the names of Chuck and Nancy for the good they do in this world.

Richman, Rabbi Chaim His bridge to the Gentile world is "Light to the Nations," P. O. Box 31714, Jerusalem, Israel. Website: www.lttn.org and e-mail at: crlight@netvision.net.il. Rabbi Richman is brilliant intellectually and one of the most humble and faithful men I know.

Salomon, Gershon is the founder of the cornerstone movement to begin work on the Temple. Temple Mount and Land of Israel Faithful Movement, P. O. Box 18325, Yochanan Horkanos 4, Jerusalem 91182 Israel. Website: www.templemountfaithful.org and e-mail at: gershon@templemountfaithful.org.

Temple Institute 24 Misgav Ladach Street, Jewish Quarter, Old City, Jerusalem. Phone: 02-894-119, Website: www.templeinstitute.org. The bookstore is simply wonderful. The Temple Institute website has beautiful photos of the Temple vessels and vestments created for the coming Temple.

Yavoh: He is Coming! The newsletter by Monte Judah from Lion and Lamb Ministries, P. O. Box 720968, Norman, OK 73070. This newsletter has wonderful insights from a Messianic Jew. Website: www.lionlamb.net and e-mail: info@lionlamb.net.

About the Author

Karen Boren was born in Salt Lake City and has lived in Montana, Idaho and California. Her first story was published when she was in the sixth grade. In junior high school her goal was to be a professional writer. Since then, she has been published in newspapers and magazines, including *Family Circle* and *Modern Maturity.* This is her first book.

A deep love of Israel has led to numerous published articles on the land of Israel, the Holocaust and biblical archaeology. Karen relished the opportunity to interview the late

Karen Boren at the West Bank religious settlement, Mitzpeh Yericho, overlooking the Judean wilderness.

Yitzak Rabin while on a press tour of Israel. She spent three weeks in the Israeli Navy in the Volunteers for Israel program. Her five trips to Israel speak of the grace of God since she was raising her family as a single mother during most of that time. She has studied Hebrew at the Jewish

Community Centers in San Francisco and Salt Lake City. Included in her library are *The Mishnah, Midrash, Zohar, Aggadah* and numerous books on Kabbalah.

A self-confessed bookaholic, Karen favors Christian writers from the late 1800s. She has a hard time finding enough bookcases to house her ever-growing library.

An abiding interest in religion has led to interviews with Hal Lindsey, Chuck and Nancy Missler, Zola Levitt, Chaim Potok, Rabbi Levi Meier and many others. Biblical archaeology and the Dead Sea Scrolls ar other subjects that intrigued Karen and led to more interviews and participation on a dig at Qumran. She co-hosted and hosted two weekly AM Radio programs on religion.

Karen has four children and five grandsons. She is a writer/editor for an essential oil/health supplement company in Utah. She welcomes comments sent to her publisher or e-mail sent to heifermaven@yahoo.com.

Index